CULTURAL COMMUNICATION IN INDIA

Concepts in Communication Informatics & Librarianship
(CICIL)

For a list of titles in this series,
see pp. 166-168 at the end of this book

Concepts in Communication Informatics & Librarianship-14

General Editor: **S.P. Agrawal**

CULTURAL COMMUNICATION IN INDIA

Role and Impact of Phonograms

J.M. OJHA
Behavioural Sciences Centre, New Delhi

CONCEPT PUBLISHING COMPANY, NEW DELHI 110059

A UNESCO sponsored project of MEDIACULT — International Institute for Audio-Visual Communication and Cultural Development, Vienna — and Behavioural Sciences Centre, New Delhi.

ISBN 81-7022-367-9

First Published 1992

Published and Printed by
Ashok Kumar Mittal
Concept Publishing Company
A/15-16, Commercial Block, Mohan Garden
NEW DELHI 110059 (India)

Lasertypeset by
Microtech Advance Printing Systems (Pvt.) Ltd.
H-13, Bali Nagar
NEW DELHI 110015

GENERAL EDITOR'S INTRODUCTION

Dr. J.M. Ojha in this concise CICIL publication draws our attention to a medium which gets overlooked in any discussion on concept and means of communication.

Phonogram in popular parlance has come to acquire a connotation different from what Dr Ojha has in mind. He uses it for phonographic records, discs and tapes. Nonetheless, phonogram has been, and is, a powerful medium in cultural communication and in this process, does play an important rôle for cultural change.

While the gramophone industry is nearing a century of its existence, the gramophone machine has all but disappeared from the drawing and living rooms, yielding place to Telly and Video. One sights them occasionally with nostalgia in period films.

However, records, in their manifestation of various *avatar*s, are enjoying an ever-increasing popularity and are good money-spinners because they entertain well and are good cultural communicators.

With their help one can understand, learn, enjoy the distinguishing features and nuances of different *Gharana*s or be inspired by the words of an enlightened soul. The cassettes come in handy during hurly-burly of an election and when situation demands can stand in for a *purohit*.

All those agencies which make such cultural communication possible through re-creation deserve our thanks as does Dr Ojha for his research effort undertaken as a UNESCO sponsored project.

S.P. AGRAWAL

FOREWORD

IN RECENT years, cultural sociology has repeatedly pointed to the fact that the technical media in general and the phonogram in particular have caused or at least initiated changes in socio-cultural processes and socio-musical structures. Popular music is unthinkable without electro-acoustic manipulation. It has its primary existence not in live performance but in the production for or recording on phonograms. The new technologies have also invaded the sphere of so-called "serious" music, causing profound changes in production, communication and reception. Unlimited reproducibility, extended repertoire, increased accessibility, a quality of performance raised to perfection, vast expansion of the music market and manifold possibilities of obtaining information about music are but a few aspects of the massive penetration of music into social reality brought about by phonogram technology.

This process has generated and still generates new variants of cultural communication. Most significant in quantitative terms is the so-called "second" way of cultural, namely technical communication which is gaining increasing importance in society. The immediate past, however, has been marked by a growing number of qualitative changes, which in their turn have repercussions on the traditional type of musical life. It is not only the habituating effect on listening expectations and listening experience that makes itself felt; research has also shown that the growing share of phonograms in musical communication is by no means bound to engender passive cultural behaviour. On the contrary, proof has been furnished that involvement in musical activities is steadily spreading not only in the sector of youth music, where a combination of musical and electro-acoustic instruments is employed, but also in conventional musical practice and in folk music. Linked with economic, legal and technical aspects, the changes in cultural communication have also occasioned mutations of cultural life. The phonographic industry, radio and television have become decisive factors in cultural life;

musical policy is gaining importance within the cultural-policy frame-works of countries. The intertwining of conventional mechanisms of musical life with new administrative-technical and economic structures and operating mechanisms has created a situation in which cultural life is increasingly determined by factors defying definition.

While MEDIACULT-research into the role of audio-visual communication in cultural development was in progress, the sector of musical communication gradually moved to the centre of attention. Numerous studies and the experience and findings derived from them lent increasing urgency to the task of investigating the role of phonograms in musical communication. All the more so, since previous work had revealed that statistics and cultural research, cultural sociology and empirical social research have done very little to shed light on this issue, in other words, that there is hardly any reliable and comparable data available.

Thanks to Mr. Ojha's study, drawn up in cooperation with MEDIACULT, research in this field, which was previously limited to Europe and North America, has now been extended to an Asian country.

The author himself said that his study "was at once difficult and challenging. Difficult, because to the best knowledge of the writer, at least initially, there was no significant compilation, documentation or statistics available except for some scattered studies. This was also the challenge".

The implementation of the project, which was impeded by a lack of Indian studies and by the size of the country must be regarded as pioneer work.

UNESCO recognised the importance of the research effort and granted a subsidy for it. MEDIACULT was able to input its own research findings and those of Dr. Ojha's study to a Council of Europe project on creativity and cultural industries.

IRMGARD BONTINCK
Director of MEDIACULT

PREFACE

THIS STUDY, jointly sponsored by the UNESCO and MEDIACULT, was at once difficult and challenging. Difficult, because to the best knowledge of the writer, at least initially, there was no significant compilation, documentation or statistics available except for some scattered studies here and there which were not enough support for a project of this nature. This was also the challenge. India has witnessed this phenomenon and experience of phonograms for about 85 years, and much of India's cultural dissemination and production in music was, if not determined, at least influenced by the gramophones. The phonograph came here not long after it was invented and used elsewhere, but here it had a different impact altogether, due to various factors – the multi-cultural diversity and still a unity, sheer size and population which made India the largest colony of British empire, a brilliant gem in her crown, and her great and ancient traditions, philosophy and civilization; all have contributed to her unique position among the comity of nations, at least much different from the up and coming countries of the West, especially the USA. It is likely that several theories, hypotheses and findings established elsewhere may have either to be rejected here or at least severely modified.

It is with this sense of challenge and fascination that the Behavioural Sciences Centre undertook to study this phenomenon of phonograms and their role in the cultural life of the country, almost from scratch. We do not know, how far we have been successful; in any case, a study of this nature and in such a vast arena is a continuous exploration and each effort unfolds something new. We have taken this study in this spirit and I hope, our sponsors and readers alike would also like to view this effort from that perspective. It offers us a great satisfaction that we have been to able to make a tangible beginning, or perhaps have added to the existing knowledge, towards a serious study of Indian cultural communication systems, spurred by the initiative of the sponsors. We are aware of several shortcomings in this – of language, construction and some overlappings, which was partly due to the nature of the subject-matter itself, and the way it was discussed. We hope we will have the benefit of the readers' indulgence.

It is obvious that a study of this nature is a teamwork and its success depends upon the cooperation and goodwill of others. It will not be proper here to single out people or organisations for the immense help they gave us for everybody helped in one way or another. Some, of course, helped us very well, giving us all the time and suggestions in spite of the severe strains this put on their time; some had their own reservations which we could easily appreciate. We are especially thankful to some old-timers and some new emerging industrialists and several artists who all helped us to make this study rich and informative. We are grateful to all of them for whatever they did for us. I must, however, thank the people directly involved, after the sponsors. Mr Shidore, the IPI Secretary was quite helpful, though he had his own limitations; so also, Dr Narayana Menon who gave us some important and useful suggestions and always was freely accessible. My especial thanks here are due to my associates, particularly Joseph Palackal, who, besides a musician and a psychologist, was a devoted worker. It is no exaggeration that without him probably the study would not have been what it is.

I have my profound thanks, however, for the UNESCO, who sponsored this study and the MEDIACULT – short for the International Institute for Audio-Visual Communication and Cultural Development – who gave me an opportunity to chart this almost unexplored area in India but which has a deep bearing on cultural communication. It need not be emphasised that phonogram in its disc form represented almost the beginning of modern mass media in the country after the print and, hence, was an important first step towards acceptance of technological culture in music and entertainment. This marked the beginning of a prolific music industry and diffusion of music. My especial thanks here are due to Dr Blaukopf – musicologist, media specialist and an accomplished musician – who inspired me by his innovative approach and full co-operation. In fact, he has been the major force behind MEDIACULT, which is now a recognised international institution for research in the concerned area. I am also thankful to Shri Ashok Mittal, Concept Publishing Company, New Delhi for bringing out this manuscript of a rather uncommon nature in a relatively unexplored area.

I hope, this gives all of us something!

J.M. OJHA

CONTENTS

LIST OF FIGURE AND TABLES

Tables

LIST OF APPENDICES

1

INTRODUCTION

AT THE turn of the century, India was ready to accept big changes. In fact, she had been accepting and assimilating big cultural changes in her vast history but now she was harnessing herself to face a new impact of so-called modern science and technology. To claim that these were entirely new influences would be wrong;[1] however, it cannot be denied that these impacts, clothed as they were in the garb of a colossal impact of the victors, prepared her to accept, and cope with, the challenge with a new determination.

There were several indications of this change: several modern universities and colleges of higher learning were being avidly used and they were preparing the people to accept the new challenges; some of our people were already distinguished scientists, for example Sir J.C. Bose had already shown, independent of Marconi, the transmission of sound through ether and many more scientists were in the making; inventions and improving technologies from the West were fast coming to this country so that at the turn of the century India already had steam engines, telegraph services, mills and factories, typewriters and printing presses to name only a few of the significant technologies of the period. It was true that these influences scratched only the surface of the social body of this vast country but it also symbolised the process which was being fast accelerated so much so that Britain would think of coronating her king in this country after a few years not only to show to the world the greatness and vastness of her empire but also with a realisation and conviction that India was now becoming ready to meet the world body of science and technology on her own. Here was a unique blend: India's ancient wisdom and culture being blended with the modern wisdom – science and technology – and a powerful culture from the west; a realisation that India was now 'coming of age' according to Britain's own standards and would press for her (India's) own identity soon. In fact, India shattered her (Britain's) wildest dreams, accelerated much faster than she thought so much so that within less than five decades India would not only free herself but would start a process of dwarfing not only the British empire but hammering the colonial ideology itself.

But that is another story!

Those were the times of grasping the hardware technology. In cultural technology also there were great upheavals. Only a few years earlier, in 1876, Edison had demonstrated his Speaking Machine; the photographs and the phenomenon of moving pictures were already being experienced. In fact, the gap between its invention and its application in India was quite narrow: the history of films in India began on July 7, 1885 with a demonstration of Lumière Brothers' Cinématograph which was shown in Paris only a few months earlier on December 28, 1884 (Barnouw and Krishnaswamy, 1980) and thence forward India would keep pace with the latest technology and use it for her own purposes. The printing presses were already churning out reading matter at a fast pace. Distances were shortening. People were experiencing this fact of change and were realising the power of hitherto unknown mass media – their private possessions had now acquired a new ability to reach larger audiences. The situation was ripe for the people to accept new changes with interest and avidity.

It was these times, bubbling with new discoveries and new ideas, when people began not only to expect but also accept rapid changes, which provided the ground for the growth of another cultural technology – the phonogram or the 'disc' – which is the subject-matter of this study. But before we describe and discuss it, it may be appropriate to have a brief sketch of the development in India of this industry itself.

The Phonogram Industry

The history of phonogram began officially in 1902 when F.W. Gaisberg sailed for India from London on September 28, 1902 (though the exports of gramophones to India had already commenced a few years earlier in 1898) as the representative of The Gramophone Co. of London with the avowed purpose 'to open new markets, establish agencies and acquire a catalogue of native records'. Even the earlier beginnings were motivated by high commercial entrepreneurship – the Victor Talking Machine Co. of

USA working since 1901 and Gramophone Co. of London working since 1898 had 'divided the globe' within themselves, and the orient came to the latter. This is how Gronow (1981) records the coming of gramophone to India. Notable narrations of its development and history have been given by Joshi in his various articles and books. (Joshi, 1977; Joshi, 1984.)

Joshi, himself a singer of repute, worked with the Gramophone Co. of India (or with the famous label, His Master's Voice, under which the company was known) for about 30 years as its Recording Officer and, therefore, has a deep personal study of the profession and the industry – its working, its motives and its operation strategy – and he has also much to say about the various artists he encountered as a representative of the company. Detailed notes in the form of an article received from him at our request narrate the development of this industry in its various aspects. We thought it worthwhile to reproduce it as it is, though it is rather long. This is reproduced as the Appendix A.

Much of what Joshi has stated, apart from mere technological and historical facts, may be his personal impressions but reading this article with others makes it clear that the most important motivation of this industry was the commercial motive. There is nothing bad about it; what is bad is that the commercial motive always or mostly superseded other and perhaps nobler motives, even in this potent cultural instrument. The phonogram was considered, in terms of Malm's two roles of phonogram (Malm, 1982), more a 'product of consumption' rather than a 'means of communication'. Thus, the Gramophone Co., in spite of being in a very envious position of having a monopoly for almost 60 years and a dominant force in years afterwards, a prestige and a world class technology, remained only a business and not a cultural force. This resulted in an utter lack of documentation or compilation of discs and consequently many recordings were lost; some master musicians never recorded and even the technology which was used were the outdated machines rejected from the west and sub-standard equipment which Joshi discovered to his utter shock when he visited the EMI studios in London in 1964 (Joshi, 1980).[2] Perhaps the greatest damage done by these was to the causes of ethnomusicology, a complete musical library or musical archives and the consequent loss of cultural heritage (Raghavan, 1953; Kunst, 1959).[3]

The history of phonograms for about 60 years before Polydor

appeared in India as a strong competitor in sixties is entwined round the Gramophone Co. now known as the Gramophone Company of India Ltd. or by its acronym GRAMCO. This change was affected after dilution of its foreign equity to 40 per cent (controlled by the EMI) in accordance with post-Independence Indian laws. No doubt, intentionally or unintentionally it, under the famous label "His Master's Voice", played an important role in making music and the consequent cultural influences accessible to the Indian public, popularising Indian music abroad and immortalising several masters.[4] But, because it remained a monopoly on the Indian scene for such a long time, it has also to bear the brunt for what could have been easily done with a little foresight and imagination, given its resources but which, unfortunately, was not done.

Most of the early companies working as feeders to the Gramophone Co. began in Calcutta, the imperial capital up to the first quarter of this century. They began around 1910 and attracted Indian talents and passed the turnover, in one way or other, to the Gramophone Co. who ploughed the profits to UK giving minimal payment to the artists. The Hindustan Recording Co., now an associate of the more recent Indian Record Manufacturing Co. Ltd., recorded the first song of Tagore.[5] It began around that time, 1910, and was also famous for its various recordings of Indian maestros, especially K.L. Saigal – music-meastro of yesteryears who reigned supreme in semi-classical music and the melody of his voice, which is still unsurpassed. Likewise, the Megaphone Co., also originating around the same period, recorded a number of contemporary masters and became especially famous for Akhtari Faizabadi, later known as Begum Akhtar, the queen of *ghazal*s. The Victoria Trading Co., which also began around that time as a trading concern,[6] is now a recording company with the same label 'Victoria' but is renamed as Vijay Radio and Gramophone Co., an IPI organization, after its commercial rights were taken over by the new purchaser in 1968.[7]

However, in course of time, most of independent organisations which had appeared or the various subsidiaries of the HMV became either closed or merged with the Gramophone Co. Some indigenous concerns which had tried to come up had to close.[8] Out of the present 16 IPI organisations, 10 are from Calcutta of which many (about 7) began around the first or second decade while the others, about 3, are of recent origin. After 1970, the first to come up was Polydor, now Music India Ltd., followed by the CBS Gramophone Records and Tapes (India) Ltd., another multi-national affiliated to the American company of the same name, in late seventies. Most other concerns, about 4 IPI and almost all non-IPIs are of recent origin and came up only during late seventies or early eighties and began operations after the cassettes appeared as the new recording technology. They explored new areas of music, had flexible marketing and bargaining strategies and many of them specialised either in a certain language, or a category of music or catered to a particular region or interest.

The first and foremost of the record pressing companies is the GRAMCO, followed by the other two multi-nationals and the totally Indian one, the Indian Record Manufacturing Co. Ltd. (INDREMA) of Calcutta. To these four, were recently added another two entirely Indian and non-IPI organisations, The Kapco International and Jyoti Record Manufacturing Co., the former at Delhi and the latter at Bombay. The Kapco is the only record pressing company in North India, with factory in Himachal Pradesh, and both of them look with high optimism towards the future of the recording industry and of discs in particular,[9] which they, along with many others, claim will be on top again. This is probably not only due to several advantages of disc-recording – better reproduction and durability – but also to some negative qualities of the existing cassette industry:

(i) low quality cassettes which are not only an irritant to sensitive listeners but also damage the instruments,
(ii) their proneness to more and speedy wear and tear, relative to the discs, and
(iii) non-availability in sufficient quantity.

The multi-nationals are incorporated companies as also many other large organisations especially in the IPI fold. However, the new companies which are medium-sized, some of them IPI members, are mostly run as individual enterprises, the common organisational structure being the partnership.

One of the recent establishments is Kusadig Recording Co. which we understand is a joint enterprise by some artists themselves, about six. This then is a new trend and shows the awareness creeping in the artists in using this medium and a realisation that they must play a more active role in the whole system not only to perhaps establish their identity as a force to reckon with but also in showing to the phonographic industry a new dimension to operate with a more cultural bent. However, it is too early to say how this experiment succeeds. In these days of cut-throat and cold-blooded competition everywhere, it requires a stupendous effort to survive and this can be done by experimenting with new ideas, discovering new talents and lines, exploring new areas of marketing and new sources for recording etc. Anyway, this is a welcome trend and apparently in line with the non-commercial recording enterprises of Sweden (Malm, 1982).

The conditions are, however, good for survival and expansion; except in film music where pirates rule the markets, several other areas are open to new entrepreneurs. The government is quite helpful though it has probably yet to realize the full cultural significance of this industry as many see it.[10] It has simplified several procedures. Exports are encouraged and for small scale cassette manufacturers there is no excise duty; there is a stringent punishment for piracy[11] and the present government is responsive to the needs of the industries' new technological demands and wants to pave the way for rapid technology transfer. So the field is open; open with challenges and also with many fascinations and a bright future[12] for different types of entrepreneurs.[13] And the end product is there – the charming, satisfying and culturally significant world of phonograms, either in cassette or disc form and perhaps both will prosper equally well. They must not only play their role as 'items of consumption' but also as 'means of communication', again to borrow the excellent role-dichotomy proposed by Malm.

NOTES

1. There is a lot of literature to prove this. A recent news item (Ghosh, 1985) may be interesting. The news items reported an exhibit, 'India: A festival of science', in Los Angeles, USA. Dr Saroj Ghosh, its creator, stated:

> Our intention was to establish that India has had a very long tradition in science and technology, at times excelling that of any other countries of the world. There's a wrong belief that whatever has been achieved in India in these areas has all been since independence (I would add: or due to the impact of the British rule - JMO). But science and technology are deeply ingrained in our culture.

There was one difference, however. The technology used was for the service of the mankind, for the welfare of the society and was accessible to the people at large; not one which was cornered by the state or some special groups for their own benefit.

2. However, he adds, 'we could not be fooled any longer . . . and embarked upon a grand plan to effect all-round development.' It is very difficult to say how much of his remarks are personal impressions and how much is the fact, though we can presume that given the commercial motives of maximum returns with minimum investment, this was largely true. The HMV studios are now equipped with some of the most modern equipment (Kuckreja, 1984). Modernisation, probably, was their response to more competition coming in and still more looming ahead in the '70s and thereafter.
3. Kunst recognises the contribution of gramophones; 'Ethnomusicology could never have grown into an independent science if the gramophone had not been invented,' but he also adds,

   > these companies, being run as they are on a purely commercial basis, have not rendered so much service to ethnomusicology as could be expected . . . They only produced records when they had reasons to expect them to be sold in quantities: in other words, they usually pandered completely to the — often regrettable — taste of the larger public and fought shy of the rarer musical expressions — forms which are being important by virtue of their being ancient . . . they (could) have rendered inestimable services to the science of ethnomusicology. . . . instead of giving (or selling) to a scientific institution the matrices of recordings which . . . have been deleted from their catalogues . . . these companies usually have destroyed them, and so, also in this way, much irreplaceable material is lost for ever.

   Raghavan, a Secretary of Madras Music Academy, (also quoted partly by Kunst) also expresses a similar disappointment in the Indian context. After suggesting that, 'more than printed materials, it is records of music that should constitute the major part of a music library,' he remarks,

   > The gramophone companies had . . . noteworthy classical renderings, but of these even the master records had been subsequently destroyed. For, the policy of the gramophone companies subsequently developed a new commercial outlook which had a bad effect on our art.

4. According to Joshi (1977), the 'present catalogue of the company includes over 7,500 records featuring every kind of fare . . . in addition to . . . recordings of educational and cultural interest.' Thus, Mahatma Gandhi, Jawaharlal Nehru were recorded; *Vande Mataram*, the national song which stirred the millions during pre-independence era, was recorded by Tagore around 1900, a copy of which was traced only in 1961. It is not an exaggeration to say that, if we forget the lapses and the motivations for the time being, diversity and richness of India's cultural (music) life may have been much poorer without the contribution of the HMV as the early pioneer. It is also true, however, that we would have flourished in many ways and probably might have done differently, probably better, without this somewhat controlling, over-powering and alien commercial (primarily, but also cultural) influence.

5. On basis of an interview with Mr Chatterjee of INDREMA, Calcutta, who met us in absence of Mr Saha, the owner who was out of the city on that day.
6. On basis of an interview with Mr K.K. Talwar, the present senior partner. It was probably established in the first decade and started operating at Lahore as a stockist of HMV and was probably known as Victoria Recording Co., with the label, 'Victoriaphone' which still continues though the owners have changed. According to another interviewee, Mr Ghosh of Megahhone, which also started around that time, it was known as 'Victoria Watch Co.'. It is possible that all these names are correct and they were changed with change in the nature of business and ownership. Another old company, Eagle Commercial Co., Calcutta also originated at Lahore and were distributors for Columbia. Such intermixing of business lines and trading was not unusual for those early days — it is not unusual even now, but more often it exists in different forms and under new terms of 'diversification' or 'departmental stores' etc. Watches and typewriters were not only the most current items 'from the West', 'fashionable' and 'status symbols' in vogue at that time, they signified a new changing work-ethos. Watches and clocks signified the changing concept of time, and dependence on clock-time — a change with far-reaching consequences — and typewriters were important tools for the 'clerk culture' that was developing or perhaps imposed by the British as a deliberate plan. Clerks were known as writers those days, and the West Bengal Secretariat at Calcutta, the imperial capital at that time, was, and still is, known as Writers' Building. This 'clerk culture,' as we all know, gradually developed into rigid bureaucratic framework and heavy paper-work by which most of us are, even now, feeling oppressed.

   Even the Gramophone Co., when established around 1902, bore the name, 'Gramophone and Typewriter Co.' (Joshi, 1984). K.L. Saigal, the legendary singer, who is still unsurpassed for his renderings, used to sell typewriters before he was discovered as a film and gramophone artist.
7. Mr K.K. Talwar is the senior partner. He was very cooperative and inspite of his work, gave enough time for information, data collection and suggestions.
8. Based upon various sources, it is estimated that between 40 to 50 labels appeared at one time or another. Some were entirely indigenous, started with ambitious plans like Young India; some were foreign investments, like Columbia and Odeon where the processing and pressing was done abroad; some small scale enterprises started as individual or family business such as Violaphone, Senola etc. For a fuller information, see Joshi (1977; 1984) and his special contribution which appears as Appendix A to this report.
9. Jyoti Records Co. is the 6th records pressing company in the country, the other 5 being GRAMCO, Music India, CBS, INDREMCO, and Kapco International. It began full operations in early 1985.

   Kapco was commissioned in March 1983. Besides pressing its own label, they press for several others, and have a very impressive record in this short time. For full details, see 'Tribute to Indira', in *Screen* of 8th March 1985.
10. Almost all respondents to Questionnaire 2, discussed in Chapter 4, opined that the government is not aware of phonogram's cultural significance or industry's problems. This was also corroborated by many industry representatives interviewed.

11. Kuckreja (1984) states how India has constantly supported and sponsored international commitments to protect intellectual property. India is a party to the Berne and Universal Copyright Conventions, and the Phonogram Convention at Geneva, 1971. At the WIPO Forum at Geneva in March 1981, India was among the 7 sponsoring countries for an anti-piracy resolution. The latest 1984 Amendment to the Copyright Act is perhaps the most stringent law in force anywhere on this issue. However, much depends upon how effectively it is supervised and implemented. The Section 5 of the Amendment reads as follows:

> . . . punishable with imprisonment for a term which shall not be less than six months but which may extend to three years and with fine which shall not be less than fifty thousand rupees but which may extend to two lakh rupees.

And the relevant excerpt from the Section 7(1):

> Any police officer, not below the rank of sub-inspector, may . . . seize without warrant, all copies of the work, and all plates used for the purpose of making infringement copies of the work wherever found.

A lakh is a hundred thousand.

12. According to the Working Group on Electronic Industry constituted by the Planning Commission for 7th plan (1986-90), the projected demand for the music industry in next five years, would be as follows (Report of the Study Team, 1984):

	in 1985-86		*in 1989-90*
Radio cassette Taperecorder	0.50 million	to	5 million
or in value	Rs. 300 million	to	3000 million
Cassette taperecorders	1.80 million	to	5 million
or in value	Rs. 650 million	to	1750 million

It was estimated that by 1989-90 there will be a demand for 300 million cassettes, C - 60 length.
(based on the background report for consideration of the 7th plan Working group. This is not the final report of the Working Group).

13. and here is what a representative of a multi-national has to say:

> . . . What the independents can do, often better than us, is produce extremely sound marketable material. I think there is a room in the world for both of us.
> - (Wallis and Malm, 1984, p. 92)

But the small industries, according to this representative, lack in that efficiency and expertise in selling and world trade, which the multi-nationals have developed. However, it is a debatable issue, what is more important: a large business with less openings for creative talents, or a small business with more openings for a better cultural communication system?

2

THE PRESENT STUDY

THE PRESENT study, proposed in 1984, was suggested by the extensive work in this area by MEDIACULT reported by Blaukopf (Blaukopf, 1977; Blaukopf, 1982) for the developed countries of the West. It was proposed to design a similar – but, as the situation vastly differs in the two contexts, not identical – study for India which may probably pave the way for such cross-cultural studies in the orient. India in several ways holds a unique position: the so-called modern technology came to us during the long colonial reign and it appears that it bears an imprint of the colossal impact of the West; India as an ancient country of the East was the largest after China but as different from her, contained within herself a large variety of cultural, religious and linguistic diversity all, however, as part of one unity. India, in a way, represented the cultural diversity in miniature yet all functionally parts of bigger units. This philosophy of smaller units contained in a larger one is, in fact, a basic dictum of Indian philosophy and her socio-cultural system. Ojha (1985) showed how the joint family concept of the Hindu social system reflects this thinking.

Unfortunately in India we do not have, to the best knowledge of this writer, any significant documentation or cultural statistics of the phonographic industry or its products compiled periodically or even as a one-time publication, as it is available in the West. I need not go into the details of citing these source materials for it will be too long an exercise as the sources are quite many and a large number of them are cited, quoted or referred by Blaukopf (1977; 1982) and Wallis and Malm (1984). Blaukopf has compiled contributions from several countries of the West which give us an idea of the large information-collection system existing there for some time. Beaud (1982) in his contribution has referred to the methodology of collecting and using cultural statistics. Such regular and systematic compilations are lacking in this country and perhaps in other regions of this part of the world as well.

In spite of this lack, or unavailability, of source material in this area, importance of the phonogram as a cultural instrument and as culture-carrier is recognised - the writer himself touched upon this in one of his pleadings for Cultural Psychology (Ojha, 1984). It was high time, it was thought, that a beginning be made towards studying this phenomenon; first, to cover the status of the industry itself as the industry was the visible carrier of technology and, secondly, to observe certain trends which may clarify to us the role of phonogram as an instrument of cultural communication. The larger questions, of course, were, how a technology affects the cultural behaviour and how the cultural influences interact.

The study reported in the following pages tries to answer these questions. Almost a complete lack of significant cultural statistics or documental sources and the extremely short time available to him led the writer to plan the study in several stages. The present attempt, incidentally, is the very first stage which opens up the possibility of further studies and promises in this fascinating area which, in turn, has ultimately to do with the socio-cultural development of the world we are living in. Our main focus was to gather some data about the existing industry which would provide a base on which we can build our inferential superstructure and raise further questions. We have tried to design this study with this objective and, given the limitations of time and resources, we hope that some inferences, information and far-reaching implications have emerged.

We have tried to discuss various aspects of the issues, as they emerged, at appropriate places and have also suggested issues for further probe. The entire study revolves round three specially designed questionnaires supplemented by some personal interviews with representatives of industry and artists besides some other significant persons such as experts, a large-scale public consumer (All India Radio) and consultants. We decided to gather the data for every year of the past decade, from 1975 to 1984, as various discussions led us to believe that the last 10 years have been the period of maximum upheavals and changes. The period saw the emergence of two multinationals, who broke the monopoly of the GRAMCO (one of which, however, began operating during 1971) and several smaller organisations and most importantly, the emergence of cassettes which has not only revolutionised the entire communication and recording system but also brought the industry face to face with its biggest problem and a tough rival: piracy and the pirate.

Instruments and Data Collection

We gathered information through 3 questionnaires seeking information about the organisational structure and business, perceptions of some representative industry personnel and the perception of artists.

Questionnaire 1, Survey of the Recording Industry in 1975-84, was the main instrument through which we obtained data from various organisations in five areas besides some factual data such as the year of establishment, composition and structure of the organisation. The nature of division and sub-division in the 5 categories are described below; the questionnaire requested an yearly break-up of such information during the 10 year (1975-84) period. These questionnaires, along with an instruction booklet were given or sent to the respondents and are reproduced in the Appendices B(i), B(ii), C and D.

Release of Programmes

This information was to be collected according to

(i) language,
(ii) semi-classical and non-classical music,
(iii) classical music, and
(iv) international music.

Non-classical music was further sub-divided into six categories:

(i) film music,
(ii) modern or semi-classical and non-classical music,
(iii) devotional music,
(iv) folk music,
(v) children's music and educational programmes, and
(vi) miscellaneous music which covered all types not included (by the respondents) in the above specified categories. (It also happened in some cases, as will be seen later, that some organisations who could not give the break-up as requested above, either according to years or according to the categories of music or both, lumped their major releases under 'miscellaneous' category.)

Similarly, classical music was bi-furcated in (i) vocal, and (ii) instrumental each for two rather distinct styles of music: the North Indian or *Hindustani* and the South Indian or *Carnatic (Karnataka)* music. We also requested the organisations to break-up the information about 'non-classical music' according to major languages. The language part was open and separate pages were provided for each language. The respondents were asked to specify the language and fill in the rest of the details as requested (Questionnaire 1: Tables I, II and III).

Production

This was divided in three columns: records, cassettes and the total. It was again sub-divided according to the music categories of the releases, namely,

(i) film,
(ii) classical,
(iii) semi-classical,
(iv) folk,
(v) devotional,
(vi) children's and educational, and
(vii) miscellaneous (Questionnaire 1: Table IV).

Sales

This sought information about the sale of pieces during the ten-year period separately for records and cassettes. No music category classification was made here (Questionnaire 1: Table V).

Import

This sought information about the master tapes imported and the country from where these were imported during the ten-year period (Questionnaire 1: Table VI).

Export

Here we sought information about the records and cassettes exported during the ten-year period and the countries whereto they were exported, split for Indian music and International music (Questionnaire 1: Table VII and VIII).

A last open section asked for suggestion and comments of the respondents. While the respondents were supposed to give the information about (1) Releases and (4) import (or master tapes) in units, information for (2) production, (3) sales, and (5) export was to be given to the nearest thousand. Release information about the International music was sub-classified for (i) popular, (ii) country, and (iii) serious music. Though these details were requested, all did not give the information in this form, mostly because it was not available so but also partly because it would have taken some time for them to rummage through old records which they were reluctant to spare.

Questionnaire 2: This was actually an interview schedule which aimed at getting the opinion and comments of some representatives of the industry about

(i) their own views about the status of the recording industry,
(ii) recording industry and the government,
(iii) relationship with artists, producers etc.,
(iv) copyright matters,
(v) import-export,
(vi) problems facing the industry, and
(vii) the future of the industry as they saw it.

An item in the end, as usual, was an open one asking the respondents to note their own comments and suggestions. This questionnaire is reproduced as Appendix C.

Questionnaire 3: This was also an interview schedule but intended for the artists. It asked for the latter's responses about various relationships which governed their association with the industry and which concerned them most such as the questions of contracts, royalty etc. The main feature of this questionnaire, however, were the 20 scaled items (scaled in the 5-pt. continuum from Strongly Agree-SA- to Strongly Disagree - SD) which were selected after some pilot interviews to elicit the opinion of the artists about the various facets of their relationship and the perception of their and industry's role in cultural development through phonograms. This questionnaire is reproduced as Appendix D. As in other questionnaires, the last item was an open one asking for their suggestions and comments.

While questionnaire 1 was sent to 43 organisations throughout the country, questionnaires 2 and 3 were administered and collected personally. The number of questionnaires returned and the places represented are shown in Table 1. Appendices E, F and G show the various organisations to whom questionnaires 1, 2 and 3 respectively were sent and the Appendix H lists various persons who were interviewed or consulted.

The 43 organisations to whom questionnaire 1 was sent were located after extensive search and information through various sources. These were spread throughout the country in distant and different centres: Calcutta and Cuttack (far east); Varanasi (north-east); Delhi, Ludhiana and Phagwara (north); Bombay (far west); and Secunderabad-Hyderabad - the twin cities, Kurnool, Bangalore, Madras and Trivandrum (south and deep south). Figure 2.1 shows the geographical locations of these places. The distances between the extreme points were about 2,000 km (east-west) and 3,000 km (north-south). As there was no regular documentation available nor any significant published material about India's music industry, it was a constant searching process to locate the producers of phonograms and pre-recorded tapes. However, an initial document by one of the industry personnel (Kuckreja, 1984) opened up to us a vision of the initial vastness of the industry, their working problems and structure and gave us a complete locatable information about the 16 members of the Indian Phonographic Industry (IPI). This information was especially interesting and useful to us, as in the beginning of the study the three most important names which came to us were of the three multi-nationals - The Gramophone Co. of India Ltd., an affiliate of EMI; The Music India Ltd. an affiliate of Polydor and the CBS Gramophone Gramophone Records and Tapes (India) Ltd., an affiliate of the US organisation of the same name-in addition to an Indian organisation of long standing, The Indian Record Manufacturing Co. Ltd. of Calcutta.

So here we found our main core of target organisations. Though not all of them were quite well-known, the document informed us of an important segment which controlled the Indian record industry in a big and organised way. They were all members of the Indian Phonographic Industry, a federation affiliated to the International Federation of Phonogram and Videogram Producers (the IFPI) which has its head-quarters in London. Locating these 16 organisations and a considerable other information given in that document by Kuckreja made possible the initial step in the direction of our

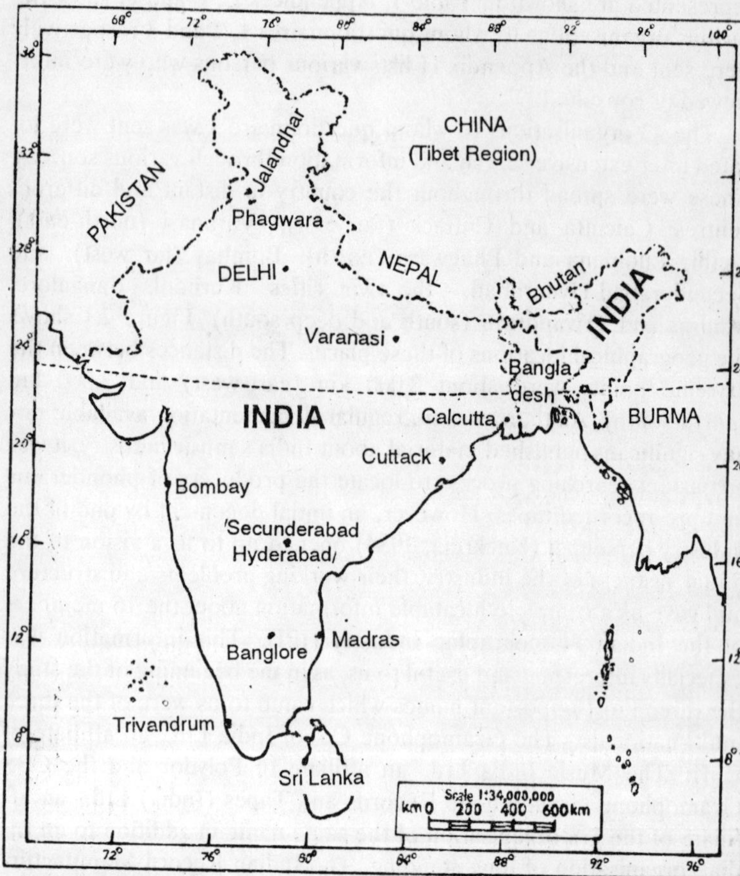

Based upon Survey of India Outline Map printed in 1987.
The territorial waters of India extend into the sea to a distance of twelve nautical miles measured from the appropriate base line.
Responsibility for correctness of internal details shown on the map rests with the publisher.

FIG. 2.1: Map of India showing the places contacted.

studying the universe which we were seeking; it also made possible a further digging in the problem by meeting and discussing with related people. This also enabled us to contact the IPI and requesting them their cooperation in this study. However, the final clearance came very late and was received only about 2 months before the scheduled time of the project delivery, in spite of the best efforts of Mr Shidore, the IPI Secretary and the letter of Miss Gillian Davis of the IFPI, London headquarters.[1]

As we initially wanted to base our study on the 16 members of the IPI, this delay not only upset our schedule but occasionally annoyed us for we could imagine, to our shock, what kind of study it would be which does not have any or much information from the giants of the industry - the 3 multi-nationals, and other Indian industries of repute. This delay, however, led us to another splendid world, the world of non-IPI members and of the artists. This came as a refreshing and relieving information and at one time we thought compensating the lack of data from the IPI industries by the rich data about the non-IPI organisations, all of whom were highly cooperative, with only a few — perhaps, only one — exceptions. We later found that many IPI members were also highly cooperative but none of them was probably ready to individually react to us as they were bound by the IPI code.

We located 27 such non-IPI organisations, most of them engaged in cassette recording but some of them also record-makers and quite a number of them were doing roaring business, specialising in thematic, regional or language songs. They had the capacity to penetrate the market of rich rural hinterlands and try unexplored areas and hence could stand well on their own. They occasionally developed their own unconventional market strategies to keep a liaison between themselves, artists and consumers. Appendix E shows the list of these 43 organisations, of which the first 16 are the IPI members, which were contacted. The list is certainly not exhaustive as many new entrants in the industry have come and more are coming. There is also an old company, Marwari Recording Co. of Jodhpur (Rajasthan) which could not be contacted due to the lack of proper address which came to us too late for any useful purpose. Similarly, there is a cultural organisation in Rajasthan, *Rupayan*, which is very much active in Rajasthani folk art and literature. We do not know whether they have any recordings or cassettes of Rajasthani folk songs or folk tales, but it is likely they may be at least getting it done under their label.

It became clear to us that only personal interviews would bring results. No one had the time or inclination, not even the IPI members, to respond to a questionnaire which on the face of it was useless to them, was asking information which was not directly helpful to them and whose filling in was only a wastage of their valuable time, as they thought it. Hence, almost all questionnaires No. 1 were completed by the writer or his associates — especially Joseph Palackal — after touring various places. The places visited included such far off places as Calcutta (1500); Bombay (1400); Hyderabad/Secunderabad (1600); Madras (2000); Bangalore (2400) and Trivandrum (3000). The figures in parentheses are the approximate distances of these cities from Delhi in kilometres. Occasionally, several trips were necessary to some of the places, especially Calcutta and Bombay.

There were exceptions, however. The GRAMCO sent to us one of the most complete documents themselves, by post and in time. This was highly satisfying to us because the GRAMCO virtually has been, and still largely is, *the* record industry in India, perhaps the largest of the organised industries, and is almost synonymous with the development of this recording technology in India and was instrumental in bringing in several masters and rich repertoire of Indian music to the knowledge of the world. In fact, any document on Indian music or its archives would not be complete without mentioning the significant contribution of GRAMCO (label, "His Master's Voice").[2] Besides GRAMCO, there were several others who returned the questionnaires themselves – 2 IPI members (N.B. Sen and Bros., Calcutta and Master Recording Co., Madras with the brand name of '*Sangeetha*') and also some non-IPI organisations. On the other extreme there were some others who either refused to fill in or did not send even though they promised to do so.[3] Some sent more or less complete data duly broken down as requested while some gave only consolidated data, either because the break-down was not available or because they did not have enough time. Appendix E also shows this information: the organisations from whom the data were received

(i) in full as requested, or
(ii) partial, that is some broken and some consolidated, or
(iii) only consolidated, that is without any break-up either in categories of music or year-wise, but just a consolidated figure for either or both of these variables.

In absence of any systematic documentation about the music industry in India, it is very difficult to say exactly what is the contribution of each recording industry to the total turnover either in release, or production, or sales or export — import but we can make certain fair guesses on the basis of data available, various newspaper reportings and some personal interviews. Inasmuch as the IPI represents the established and organised sector and traditional companies of long duration we will mainly follow this division; hence, the analysis which follows largely splits the information according to the IPI and non-IPI organisations. However, this does not under-rate in any way the importance of non-IPI sector, qualitatively or quantitatively.

Though we have followed this division for convenience and other reasons stated above, it may also be kept in view that whereas most of non-IPI organisations are of relatively recent origin — some as late as 1984, though the majority originated in late seventies or early eighties — most of the IPI organisations have been existing for long, since about the first decade of the century. Of the recent units two are multi-nationals and by their very nature and size of resources they are quite dominating. Of others, about 5 or 6 are of recent origin and of relatively middle-size resources and operations, and combine trading with the recording — trading not necessarily limited to their products but also covering other items of electronic music industry as well. We may also keep in view the fact, that out of the 16 IPI members, only 9 responded and of the three multi-nationals therein only one — the GRAMCO.[4]

Limitations of the Study

The first limitation of this study was the time. As explained earlier, the time available (about 6 months, later extended to about 8) was already quite insufficient for such a study considering the vastness of the country, absence of any previous studies of this type, lack of documentations and the respondents' initial hesitation to give the information due to various reasons. This handicap was further aggravated by the extreme delay in the clearance by the IPI Executive. Hence, in spite of our intention to take a wider and more scattered sample, we had to be satisfied only with a sample available to us, but after as thorough a search as possible in the circumstances. Given more time and a fuller information from a wider sample, we would have liked to have subjected this study to a more rigorous scientific methodology and experimental design, rather than just limiting it to a simple survey.

We also do not know how far the organisations included here represent the industry as a whole or what is the extent of their share in the turnover but we have a feeling that the universe covered by these 22 respondent organisations probably gives us a good indication of the total picture. We may not draw general conclusions but broadly guess the contribution the industries make in the growth of products and markets, and in playing their role in cultural dissemination. The generalisation is also difficult due to a vast unreported and unknown area – the area of pirates – which control anywhere between 90 per cent and 95 per cent, or more according to some, of the total share of cassette sales. Especially in film music it was the consensus of many that the largest consumers of the records are pirates[5] because the quality of reproduction is better from records than from cassettes and the records are lifted immediately for multiplication just as soon as they are released.

The industries represented in the analysis also represent among themselves various types of structures – incorporated, partnerships or just individual enterprises; large and small; national or multinational; organised and not-so-organised. The interviews with the representatives of industry, though are not many, reflect to our pleasure and surprise a variety of some serious thinking and motivations about their roles, and problems and future of the industry. Some of these reflections go beyond just the thoughts of hard-boiled commercial minds. Hence, this sample, it is hoped, gives us a wide spectrum of various ideologies, practices and beliefs. However, inspite of this, it is a severe limitation and the results have to be judged in that light.

I think the value of this study lies in the area it opens up for studying the various strategies and aspects of cultural industry and cultural policy in this part of the world, the role that cultural industries have played or are playing and the growth of this industry as a determinant and also a consequence of public/consumer behaviour, and more importantly, the status of the artist in this whole system. This study, therefore, is likely to point to several issues which may, perhaps, be more fruitfully further probed, researched or just surveyed.

NOTES

1. The delivery date originally scheduled was Sept. 30, 1985. The IPI clearance

was received by us in the 1st week of August. The Secretary, Mr Shidore was highly interested in the project from the beginning but as this was an executive matter, it needed a final clearance by the executive, and this took time. However, once the clearance was received, it was relatively an easy task to get the cooperation from members, though none except a few returned the questionnaire voluntarily. Most information was collected in person, by going to the places. There were few, on the other extreme, who either did not give the information or did not send it even after promising so in a personal call. These are risks in a data-collection situation, which is a good information by itself.

2. A brief write-up about the company, sent to us by them, appears in Appendix J. Also see note 4 of Chapter 1.
3. — e.g. a multi-national felt, it was not worth spending time for this type of work. He could not spare his staff for this as there was no return, but could extend the service if some definite steps were taken to solve the problem of piracy. Another multi-national promised to send the information which was never received. Some IPI organisations from Calcutta promised to send the information which was never received. An IPI member from Varanasi was neither personally contacted nor did he respond. All non-IPI organisations who were contacted, did give the information on spot or later sent it, except one or two. The rest of the non-IPI organisations to whom this request was made either replied, or did not reply, but did not say, 'no.'
4. See note 5 of Chapter 1 for an explanation how some of the early organisations began as traders in general merchandise, especially, watches and typewriters. Even GRAMCO began as 'Gramophone and Typewriter Co.' Joshi felt that a gramophone and a typewriter are somehow related. A typewriter types words and the gramophone record has words and sound etched on it by a process of recording.
5. On basis of several interviews: One interviewee expressed optimism for the record industry, which was not going down because of a perceptive audience, though its percentage is very small. However, pirates remained the biggest consumers and also steady ones for they needed records to copy songs. . . into cassettes. According to one, only 5 per cent of the records go to real consumers.

3

ANALYSIS AND FINDINGS-I

WE WILL begin with the Questionnaire 1 through which we collected the data from the respondent organisations regarding: (i) releases, (ii) production, (iii) sales, (iv) import, and (v) export. This will be followed by an analysis of the responses received to the Questionnaire 2 which will indicate how some of the industry personnel themselves look at various aspects affecting the industry, such as copyright, relationship with artists, government's role, and also how they look towards the future. These responses have been discussed under the heading, 'Status of the Industry'. We will supplement this with 'comments' which is the information we have gathered from various sources, such as interviews and other documents. Questionnaire 3, as was already explained earlier, tries to probe how the artists themselves look at their relationship with the industry and tries to know their views about related matters. These will be discussed under the heading, 'Status of the Artists' to highlight the perception of artists in relation to the phonogram and the phonographic industry.

As stated in the last chapter, we will, wherever possible, split the actual data we have received among the IPI and non-IPI organisations. However, we may stress again, this does not under-rate the growing importance, qualitatively and quantitatively and also in size of business, of the non-IPI organisations who are penetrating the market in a big way and are exploring sources and markets so far untouched or tapped only minimally and are experimenting with new marketing strategies. Mention may also be made of several non-IPI organisations who are now fast eroding the monopoly of the IPI organisations, especially of the multi-national ones, in several areas of music, especially film music. Mention may also be made here of the pirate 'T-series' brand which 'have firmly entrenched into the market' (Kuckreja, 1984) and which, we understand, controls 80 per cent or perhaps much more than that of the pre-recorded cassette market for the film music and is probably the most threatening single factor.

(According to our information, the business is now fully legalised and registered with well-run studios and production facilities with offices at Delhi and Hyderabad).

Releases

Tables 2 to 12 present this information arranged in various ways to show the contribution of IPI and non-IPI respondents to the total number of releases, according to the categories of music and also according to languages. This arrangement, according to the languages and categories, was deemed necessary as it would illustrate a trend how the musical interest of the population is being tapped and how the languages are being used more and more. It also helps us in inferring the role and the market of traditional music producers and of the emerging non-IPI music industry. No splitting of the IPI and non-IPI organisations was done for the classical music (Tables 11 and 12) as the contribution of non-IPI respondents in this category was much less — almost insignificant and in any case they come after 1980 and that too in some releases of regional music. Even among the IPI members, the organisation which has contributed the most in production of classical music is perhaps one — the GRAMCO. The other multi-nationals — CBS and Music India — and some other organisations may also be having quite sizable lists but they have not reported. As far as we understand, the major emphasis of the non-respondent IPI organisations is on the popular forms of semi-classical music especially the *Ghazals*, a music with lyrical quality which is becoming very popular not only in India but also abroad, and also devotional music.

We can now summarise our findings about releases as follows:

1. IPI members still hold about 78 per cent share of the total releases in the country (Table 8). The share is certainly falling — from 98.30 per cent in 1976 with slight yearly variations. Thus, up to 1977-78, the share of the IPI organisations was almost 100 per cent, gradually dropping afterwards while the share of non-IPI organisations was gradually increasing from a mere 2.7 per cent in 1975 to a running average of 13.46 per cent at the end of the ten-year period. This shows a good hold of IPI organisations but also indicates a gradual penetration by the non-IPI organisations. We note a gradual decline in IPI

performance after 1981, perhaps under the impact of cassettes and emergence of more companies with a big drop in last two years. This trend is also reflected in the actual number of releases during the period. The sudden drop in the number of releases in 1982 points, perhaps, to a sudden sense of 'shock' and 'bewilderment' at the dramatic emergence of the cassettes and the pirates and the rapidity with which they captured the market, all of which may have put the entire industry out of gear for the moment. That this was one of the likely reasons is evidenced by the fact there has been a slight recovery in the following year.

2. Considering the categories of music, (non-classical) we find that,

   (i) in *film music*, the IPI members, though dominating, have come down very much from 100 per cent, up to almost 1980, to about 67.43 per cent in 1984 (Table 9). There is a steep drop in early eighties but only in 1984 they seem to be picking up. There is a corresponding increase — and a remarkable upward trend in case of non-IPI organisations who at the end of 1984 held about one-third share of the film music. This is the picture which emerges from our sample but we may keep in view that much of the film music releases reported here by IPI members belong to *Hindi* language film music mainly by one company — the GRAMCO — up to at least 1980 and much of it afterwards also. The two other multi-nationals have not been included. While the share of the CBS in film music may not be much as it mainly concentrates on popular semi-classical music (*Ghazal*s etc.) and international music, the Music India seems to have captured a sizable share. Another company which already dominated the sales market and which is now coming up as far as releases are concerned, is the 'T-series'— already mentioned earlier — which is not represented here. The rest of the IPI and non-IPI organisations mainly share in the production of regional film music.

   (ii) It is in the *Devotional and Children's music* that the penetration of non-IPI organisations seems remarkable. This is a new welcome trend showing the change in the marketing behaviour — the up and coming industries are penetrating in areas which were more or less left neglected by the established IPI organisations. This also point to the emergence of regional forms, as also the emergence of new artists because while the established IPI organisations, especially the multi-nationals, do have restrictive policies — now of course becoming flexible — the non-IPI organisations experiment with new strategies to tap the unconventional sources and markets.

3. The above observations about dominance of film music and emergence of other forms can also be corroborated from Table 4 which shows that out of a total of 15025 releases during the past 10 years, 8681 or 57.78 per cent was film music. It is in this area that most piracy occurs. The other categories which are now emerging are Devotional (2036/15025 or about 13.50%) and Semi-classical (1280/15025 or about 8.50%) followed by other categories. We can see that these other forms have strengthened their position from an insignificant proportion in 1975 to quite a sizable proportion in 1984, both numerically and proportionately, with slight yearly variations.

However, we observe from Table 10 that in spite of an excessive increase in the actual number of releases, the growth in percentage is quite slow. In fact, it appears (without any testing for the significance of differences) that while the growth in percentage is almost insignificant there is a stupendous numerical growth. This may be interpreted in many ways but one plausible interpretation is to account this to the spontaneous growth in the market due to the increase in sources (films etc.) without any endeavour on the part of organisations towards a calculated speciality growth.

4. The film-music dominates the recording industry in almost all languages except in Punjabi and Rajasthani. Some of the likely reasons are:

   (a) that the film activity is largely concentrated in the west, south and east representing the

      (i) Marathi-Gujarati,

(ii) Tamil, Telugu, Kannada and Malayalam, and

(iii) Bengali, Assamese and Oriya regional languages respectively. Hindi being a language spoken by the majority, a national link language and understood by a vast number, is the language of most films produced in Bombay and for several years now also the South (Madras). Calcutta was a pioneer in film industry and had produced a number of Hindi quality and epoch-making films but it has now become mostly limited to regional films, majority of them in Bengali.

(b) Punjab and Rajasthan, both rich in folklore and devotional music, do not have any film studio though efforts are being made in this direction. Films in these languages are also produced in Bombay which has been the traditional film capital of India, now sharing this position with Madras. The number of films produced in these languages also is not high and, hence, the film music output is not much — whereas the recording itself is not bound by these limitations.

5. Table 10 gives further important information: that the share of film music in the total release has been gradually dropping and in 1984 it has dropped steeply, from 62.27 per cent in 1975 to 38.24 per cent in 1984. Some reasons for this drop may be: (i) diversion of film music to other non-respondent organisations, and (ii) consolidated report given by some companies which clubbed all music in 'miscellaneous' category, though this is unlikely to have much effect because such organisations have been mostly active in non-film recording.
6. As far as language is concerned, we see emergence of regional languages especially the 4 major South Indian languages. While Hindi attracts most releases, the South Indian languages are picking up, at least numerically, as the over-all percentage through the years does not seem to vary much inspite of annual fluctuations.
7. Table 6 (distribution of releases according to the music categories) gives us the following information:

(i) that about 25 per cent of the total releases during the ten-year period are in Hindi (25.85%) followed by Tamil (12.94%), Telugu (13.24%), Bengali (9.54%), Punjabi (7.34%) and Kannada (7.12%).

(ii) However, the proportion differs when we consider according to language and the music categories:

(a) largest percentage of *film songs* is in Hindi (34.36%), followed by the 4 South Indian languages: Telugu (18.09%), Tamil (14.48%), Malayalam (9.12%) and Kannada (8.79%).

(b) in *semi-classical music*, the largest recorded language is Urdu (48.66%), followed by Bengali (26.26%) and Hindi (6.84%). It may be mentioned here that Urdu has become quite popular due to the extensive popularity of *Ghazals*; Bengali has also a large variety of songs and music which is being explored now; in fact, Bengal has always been in forefront of musical recordings of its own rich heritage.

(c) in *folk songs*, the largest percentage is in Punjabi language (46.60%), followed by Hindi (9.97%), Bengali (10.52%) and Rajasthani (6.42%). As explained above, different regions of India have rich traditions of folk music. In most of the languages, there is abundant film-production and it nearly overshadows production of other types of music and occasionally the film music overlaps with other varieties. In Rajasthani and Punjabi, where film production is low, the folk music is becoming the emergent and prominently recorded music.

(d) in *devotional songs*, the largest percentage is in Tamil (25.30%) followed closely by Punjabi (21.39%), and Hindi (14.60%), Kannada (10.88%) and Telugu (7.87%).

(e) in *children's and educational programmes*, though they are numerically not many, Hindi (32.81%) is followed by Bengali (18.75%), Marathi (14.06%) and Gujarati (9.38%).

(f) majority of *miscellaneous* songs (not covered above but excluding classical music) are in Bengali (41.04%), followed by Hindi (41.90%), Oriya (10.89%) and Telugu (10.34%). This category, however, is elusive because several organisations have given consolidated figures in music categories even though they might be falling in one of the specified categories. As far as possible we have followed the classification given by the reporting organisations where it was so given. The category of 'other' languages have not been considered above because it represented many minor languages with insignificant numbers and, moreover, the language was not specified by the reporting organisation.

We may write here about *Urdu* also. *Urdu* has got a special character. It is neither a regional language nor a community language (of Muslims, as is generally believed). Due to its national character and resemblance to Hindi, many films which have dominant *Urdu* music or language are perhaps classified as Hindi e.g. a style of semi-classical music, the *Ghazal*s, are now popular music styles and lyrics which are set to tunes. Though the grammar of Hindi and Urdu are distinct, these two languages have blended so well (mostly due to (i) predominant Hindu-Muslim mixed culture in North India, (ii) long reign of Muslims, and (iii) *Urdu* being the court language during the later Mughal rule and also used for a considerable period by the British) that it is sometimes very difficult to distinguish the two spoken languages.

8. Table 7 (distribution of releases according to languages) gives us the following information:

   (a) in *Hindi*, the film music is recorded the most (83.40%), followed by devotional songs (7.64%),
   (b) in *Gujarati*, also the film songs/music is recorded the most (68.11%) followed by devotional music (14.75%),
   (c) in *Marathi*, again film songs are recorded the most (52.47%), followed by devotional music (15.29%), and semi-classical music (14.59%),
   (d) in *Punjabi*, the largest percentage of recorded music is devotional music (39.42%) closely followed by Folk music (37.76%) and film (15.50%),
   (e) in *Rajasthani*, also the largest percentage belongs to the folk music (66.20%) followed by devotional (11.27%),
   (f) in *Bengali*, the largest recorded music belongs to the

'miscellaneous' category (31.43%) closely followed by film music (30.15%) and semi-classical music (27.34%). A large number of music also belongs to folk category (10.56%). It is interesting to note that in this language no one category far exceeds the next largest, and all are almost equally represented. We may not consider 'Folk' and 'Miscellaneous' as quite distinct categories as many titles might overlap, or the classification may be ambiguous,

(g) in *Assamese*, the largest percentage of recorded music belongs to film music (41.89%) followed by semi-classical (20.27%), and miscellaneous (22.97%),

(h) in *Oriya*, again it is the film music which is at the top (42.53%) followed by semi-classical (36.21%) and devotional (13.79%),

(i) In *Tamil*, again the film music tops (70.23%) followed by devotional (26.44%),

(j) in *Telugu*, again the film music is predominant (85.76%) followed by devotional (8.04%) and miscellaneous (5.71%). It is evident, however, that film music far exceeds any other music,

(k) in *Malayalam*, again the film music tops (92.27%) almost to the exclusion of any other. The next two categories are devotional (5.90%) and miscellaneous (1.57%) which are almost insignificant as compared to the film music,

(l) in *Kannada*, again the film music tops (75.86%) though not as much as in other South Indian languages. The next category is devotional (20.22%).

(m) in *Urdu*, the semi-classical music is almost exclusively recorded (98.68%). As explained earlier, *Ghazal* is the most popular music-style. Usually, it is considered as an Urdu composition, though all lyrics may not be as Persian-saturated as some of the classical *ghazal*s are and many of the modern lyrics may be quite easy to follow as an easily understandable Hindi-Urdu mixture but still it will be classified as Urdu composition. In the same way there are a number of other categories in Urdu, such as *Naat*s and *Qawwali*s, the former of which is the devotional music. We presume, that all *Urdu* compositions are considered as semi-classical irrespective of any special classification. Likewise, many of the film music, which may be either

Urdu or a mixture of Hindi-Urdu is classified as Hindi film, or Hindi semi-classical.

Taking an over-all average, we find that the releases of film music far exceed other releases (62.73%). The next important categories are devotional music (13.52%) followed by semi-classical music (9.97%). Film music tops for *Hindi, Gujarati, Marathi, Assamese, Oriya*, and all the four major South Indian languages, *Tamil, Telugu, Malayalam* and *Kannada* with slight variations here and there. The four South Indian languages are the regional languages of Tamil Nadu, Andhra Pradesh, Kerala and Karnataka states respectively. In *Bengali*, film music shares the top honours with the semi-classical music, while in *Punjabi, Rajasthani* and *Urdu*, the folk-devotional, folk and semi-classical music outstrips the film-music releases respectively. In *Urdu*, there is no film music reported; perhaps this means that several *Urdu* compositions in films are classified in Hindi language.

Releases in Classical Music

Indian classical music is broadly divided in two distinct types — North Indian or *Hindustani* and South Indian or *Carnatic* (*Karnataka*) though the latter is not limited to Karnataka state only as the name implies. Though basically they are the same, originating from the same ancient sources and have an identical structure, notation system, system of melodies (*Raga*), and of timing (with slight variations), the manifestation, style of singing and expressions are distinct. While the North Indian music was influenced and enriched by great masters from different cultures, especially Islam and became music in different settings giving expression to various situations, Carnatic music more or less kept its purity through the generations, is rich in semi-tones and is mostly devotional.

Tables 11 and 12 show the releases in Hindustani and Carnatic music. As the contribution of non-IPI organisations is extremely small, the Table 11 presents the consolidated information received from the 10 respondent organisations. The others did not report anything. Even of the 3 IPI members, the largest contribution is of the GRAMCO though the other multi-nationals (but non-respondents) have also begun to add some of these titles to their catalogues, especially the Music India. Out of these 10, one gave a consolidated figure and Table 11 shows this separately. Table 12 shows the contributions of the 3 different types of organisation to give an idea of their share in the total releases. The tables are self-explanatory and need only a little explanation.

(i) The GRAMCO's share in releases of Hindustani music especially in records (both vocal and instrumental) is almost total though it is giving way to others in cassette programmes. Anyway, GRAMCO's share in the total releases of Hindustani music (considering both records and cassettes) is still impressive: 74.38 per cent (241/324). In Carnatic music, GRAMCO is giving way to others so that its total share during the ten-year period is only 34 per cent (119/350). The over-all average, however, shows that GRAMCO still controls 53.41 per cent (360/674) share of all classical releases.

(ii) The number of releases are not much as compared to other types of music, probably because of limited market and limited expertise but also partly due to the loss or non-existence of many recordings. It may also be due to the reluctance of established organisations to encourage or attract new talents and thus take a marketing risk, and, hence, the recording organisations bank more on established experts and professionals.

(iii) It is likely that the full richness of the Indian classical music, which takes time to 'unfold' itself, is not much amenable to the rigid controls of the recording technology and, hence, they are no substitute for 'live' performances which are not so 'imprisoned' by several constraints. This difference is felt by the master-performers and also the connoisseurs of music. Consequently, this affects the market consumption. It is much better now than before, when only 3 minutes and 20 seconds were allowed for a 78 rpm recording, but still the constraints are there and this may be a factor which may be interfering with a full expression ultimately resulting in a psychological resistance, both by artists and consumers.

(iv) The trend is not distinctly visible and it seems that the classical music will suffer not so much due to other types of music but due to the absence of those conditions which encouraged creation, performance and enjoyment of this type of music (Kumar, 1985; Ojha, 1985), unless some risks are taken which, perhaps, is too much to expect from commercial organisations. Suitable policy-measures for its preservation, documentation and encouragement are likely to widen the consumer base which may offer a suitable attraction to the commercial companies for taking this risk.

Production

Tables 13-A, 13-B, and 13-C present this information for 2 IPI members and 8 non-IPI organisations. While one IPI member, The Master Recording Co., Madras with the label 'Sangeetha' gave a detailed break-up, the other one, the GRAMCO combined some categories other than (i) film, (ii) semi-classical, and (iii) classical in the 'others' category. This made the task of showing the total production turnover difficult. We, therefore, preferred to split this information in Tables 13-A, 13-B and 13-C, in order to show the contributions of these organisations and also to show how regional organisations are responding to the market and consumer needs.

These three tables lead us to following inferences:

(i) that production in film music surpasses any other in GRAMCO (60.98%) which had the monopoly in film music up to only recent times (Table 13-A). Film music is also the largest combined production (56.81%) of the 8 non-IPI organisations which mostly cater to regional (South Indian) music. One IPI organisation (Table 13-B) which also caters to the regional music in South, however, produces more devotional music than film (57.18%) of the total production for the former compared to 27.55 per cent of the latter).

(ii) the conglomeration of 8 non-IPI organisations also produce a large number of devotional music (31.32%) though much less than the film music (56.81%). As they mostly cater to a regional market, it is evident from this information, along with the information given by Table 13-B (of the large production in devotional music by an IPI member) that, except in Hindi which is the speciality of Table 13-A, the producers are, perhaps, responding to the people's need for devotional music. This can also be interpreted differently: that the new up and coming producers see the devotional music as, perhaps, the most potent category which can influence the people and change the consumer behaviour which they may exploit to penetrate the established markets more forcefully.

(iii) the cassette production is showing an increasing trend in all music categories and all organisations. This is more evident in case of one IPI organisation and the 8 non-IPI organisations who almost exclusively depend upon this technology. The GRAMCO (Table 13-A) produces more records though we can see a gradual shift to cassettes until, in 1984, the cassette production almost equals the record production in film music and actually exceeds in classical, semi-classical and international music while the records have a larger production in other types of music. International music, it may be noted, is usually imported as Masters from their principal collaborators abroad.

(iv) It is obvious from the consideration of these tables that while film music still dominates due to various reasons, many of them quite obvious, the devotional music is emerging as the next dominating type. This corroborates very well the analysis of releases which also brought out the importance of devotional music as the leading music category after films. In fact, the figures in Table 13-B give us some startling information: that while in 1976 and 1977 there was almost no production of devotional music cassettes (perhaps this was an experimental period to gauge the market reaction), the year 1978 saw a stupendous increase by 172 times! (from 0.1 thousand in 1976 and 1977 to 17.2 thousands in 1978). This may be partly due to emergence of more non-IPI organisations around this time but also due to a firm conviction of the producers that this was the music which would not only open new avenues for them but will also face the challenge of film music and other established organisations. During the 6 years, from 1978 onwards, the production increased 3.5 times (from 17.2 thousands in 1978 to 60.4 thousands in 1984). It seems that many organisations started with this area in mind and added other lines afterwards.

Sales

Table 14 presents this information split between 5 IPI and 9 non-IPI organisations who reported these figures. The table leads us to the following observations:

(i) that IPI members still hold a monopoly of the total sales (97.35%). In this connection we may mention that the two multi-nationals who have not responded, Music India and the CBS, also hold a substantial share of the sales.[1] The share in sales of the IPI members was reduced from about 100 per cent up to 1978 (7740/7826.2) to 92.20% in 1984 (6459.2/7005.65), while the share of non-IPI organisations rose correspondingly during the same period from 1.10 per cent (86.2/7826.2) to 7.80 per cent (546.45/7005.65). This indicates that, as far as sales are concerned, the total share of the IPI members is falling but falling so slow that it looks almost steady over the years with slight insignificant variations.

(ii) that IPI members relied on records initially but from 1978 onwards when they began to produce cassettes, increasingly sold them so that by 1984 the sale of cassettes was much higher than the records (3760 thousand cassettes as against 2699.2 thousand records). The same applies to the non-IPI organisations who, at least many of them, began their existence by selling cassettes along with records but ended by primarily depending upon the cassettes up to 1981, when they also began selling more records, so that by 1984 their sales of records were only slightly lower than that of the cassettes (263.95 thousand records as against 282.5 thousand cassettes). This is evidenced by the fact that a number of record-pressing non-IPI organisations — at least 2 — have come in existence during this period besides the 4 IPI members already existing for recording-pressing — 3 multi-nationals and one Indian. Obviously, these two new non-IPI record-pressing companies would not have ventured in this unless they envisaged a bright future for the records.[2]

(iii) for the IPI members, the figures during the 10-year period show declining sales in records, lowered by about 45 per cent between 1975 and 1984 (from 4882 thousand to 2699.2 thousand in 1984) while the sale of cassettes increased by about 80 times in 7 years (from 47 thousand in 1978 to 3760 thousand in 1984). In non-IPI organisations, on the other hand, we see a different, almost opposite trend. The record sales were almost steady, and insignificant, for 7 years up to 1981 but in 1982 there was an increase by about 80 times in record sales, which almost doubled in 1983 and more than tripled in 1984, while the sales of cassettes just about doubled within 6 years (from 116.1 thousand in 1979 to 282.5 thousand in 1984). This probably indicates an interest on the part of new-comers to fill in the gap being gradually created by the IPI members who are, apparently, shifting to cassettes.

(iv) from the total figures we find that during the ten-year period under consideration, the IPI members sold many more records than cassettes while the non-IPI organisations sold many more cassettes than records. This supports our earlier contention that records do have a stable market and, in many cases, they are probably preferred by people. This also points to an encouraging outlook for the records inspite of the reports that cassettes are threatening the production and sale of records. While this may be true of some specific categories of music such as film music, we may not generalise this. It may be worthwhile, therefore, to seek the reasons for low sales of records elsewhere than exclusively, or even mainly, in the cassette boom. For example, this may be due to the high prices of records themselves, high prices of record-playing instruments and equipment, and their relative non-portability.[3]

Import

We asked for the number of master tapes imported and the countries from where these were imported. Only two organisations GRAMCO, an IPI member, and a non-IPI member reported that they imported but the former did not supply the figures as they were not available with them, while the other one did supply. The others did write that they were not importing and the two multi-nationals, who we believe import a number of masters through their principals abroad, did not respond at all, as already reported earlier. Western music is becoming quite popular in India, especially with young people in addition to the foreigners who provide a regular market for such music. A special programme of western music is regularly broadcast by the All India Radio, while it is also a part of several other programmes.

Table 15 shows the figures reported by only one non-IPI organisation. This organisation, started about 10 years back, is an individual concern and an emerging middle-sized company. In absence of any other comparative data, we are unable to deduce anything except that imports are declining over the years, at least for this organisation, though we believe that this is not the fact. They might be declining but not at the rate evidenced by the above table. Besides these legitimate imports, there are immense unauthorised imports of pirated cassettes from abroad, especially from the Far East and Gulf countries. The size of such business, however, cannot be known — it can only be guessed.

Export

We understand that the GRAMCO is the largest, if not the only, organisation to import Indian and International music to other countries. The latter music, as we will soon see, is exported mostly to the East European countries. Indian music is becoming quite popular abroad and it will not be wrong to assume that substantial exports are made by several organisations of which only a few have reported here. Indian immigrant population in several countries want to hear their own music and there is a growing trend to appreciate Indian music. It is possible that several exporters may be principally catering to some specific segments of Indian population with their regional music.[4] Though only 5 organisations have reported these figures, 7 have stated that they export while some others are working out procedures for doing so (Appendix I).

Tables 16-A and 16-B relate to export. Table 16-A shows the export figures of GRAMCO which is the largest exporter of the respondent organisations, and has been exporting to various countries over the years. Table 16-B shows the contribution to exports of several other organisations — all non-IPI members, of relatively recent origin. Indian music is becoming increasingly popular and the government policy encourages export though some are concerned about the retarding influence of lengthy paperwork and other procedures.[5]

Tables 16-A and 16-B lead us to make the following observations:

(i) that the largest exports are made to the countries where there is large Indian population — the U.K. being at the top followed by North America which includes Canada. The countries in the second largest group are South America, West Europe and the Far East where a reasonably large Indian population has settled and/or is working.

(ii) the exports seem to be declining over the years. This may be due to pirated cassettes being marketed or produced in the destination country itself, especially in the Far East where most pirated cassettes originate and from where they are also imported in India by several dubious means.

(iii) An interesting trend which the author observes is that the records do have, more or less, a stable market abroad. One of the reasons for this preference of records to cassettes in the foreign market may be due to the pricing — the difference in the prices of records and cassettes may not be wide enough or at least is not felt as wide enough to tempt people to prefer cassettes to records unless they have a special reason to do so. Of the total exports reported here — 10,834 — only 10 per cent are cassettes while 90 per cent are records, which is a staggering figure compared to the Indian market. This supports our contention that the record industry is not going down much: besides the bright future many see for the records in India itself, the reduced consumption of records here is being much more than compensated by international demand and exports, in its stead.

(iv) that East Europe is emerging or rather emerged as a large and steady export market for Indian records and cassettes especially for International music. Here also we see the prepondering consumption of records to the preference of cassettes. The export to these countries is showing a developing trend, inter alia, due to the special trade treaties with India which facilitate the inter-commerce and also due to the relative restrictions in trading with developed countries. Moreover, the socialist countries, because of their emphasis on inter-cultural understanding, are probably showing increasing appreciation of music from India.

We now end our discussion based on the analysis and findings of the Questionnaire 1. For the sake of convenience and to avoid this chapter being too long, the responses to Questionnaires 2 and 3 with our comments will be discussed in the next chapter — a continuation of the present one.

NOTES

1. On basis of interviews and other information, the Music India started as

Polydor in 1971, changed to Music India Ltd. in 1975. It has 25 per cent of the market share. Produced only records till 1980, started proucing cassettes from 1981. Now the ratio is 25 records to 75 cassettes. 10 to 15 releases every month. Peak years of the company were 1975-77. Joshi (Appendix A) relates how it came to India through the well-known dealer in photo and cine goods possessing a cine-film processing laboratory: the Patels of Bombay. According to a report in '*Update*' by Basu (1985) while the HMV was the first to introduce *Ghazals*, it is the Music India who reaped the benefits; *Ghazals* amounts to about 40 per cent of Music India's current earnings.

CBS, started in early eighties, began with international music, but also included Indian films, and *Ghazals*, the latter remaining their special repertoire. Also a little devotional music. Cassettes amount to almost exclusive production — about 99 per cent. CBS exports International music, chiefly to East European countries.

2. See note 9 of Chapter 1, which refers to a news report about Kapco, in 'Screen' of 24th March 1985. Some more details from that report are: The Director Mr S. Kapoor is a graduate from Film and TV Institute, Poona. They manufacture about 30,000 records per month, and press for several other labels. Kapco was commissioned in March 1983.
3. Several interviews suggest that records will have a steady market, and perhaps their consumption will grow. According to one, it can prevent piracy to certain extent for records are difficult to copy. Some have opined that one of reasons for the popularity of records outside India is their low price (as felt by them) in addition to the sound quality of the recording which only records can give.
4. – e.g. *Amritvani* (Delhi) specialises in Punjabi language programmes, majority of which is devotional (in Sikh religion). About 15 per cent is exported to UK catering to the Sikh community there during the last 5 years.
5. This is more or less a steady grievance of many exporters as is evident from the responses to questionnaire 2. An exporter who was interviewed stated, that there were so many restrictions that it would seem that the Government does not want anybody to export. He agreed that there should be a quality control on export goods but the procedure has to be made simpler. 'The process is too tedious', 'it takes about a month to clear all formalities', and 'it is no incentive at all'. It was agreed, however, that good incentives are being offered for export.

4

ANALYSIS AND FINDINGS-II

Status of the Phonogram Industry

THIS SECTION deals with various issues affecting the industry in general, namely,

(i) motivational urges and general outlook,
(ii) its relationship with the government,
(iii) its relationship with the artists,
(iv) copyright matters,
(v) import-export strategy and policy,
(vi) problems, and
(vii) a look towards the future.

This information was collected through the Questionnaire 2 intended for the industry personnel. In all, 9 questionnaires were returned. As this is too small a figure, no attempt has been made here to draw any conclusion or to derive percentages except that we assume that the replies indicate a sort of brain-storming and express the significant concerns and the thinking of the industry. We will discuss the responses received but it will be followed by our 'comments' based on interviews and available information. The list of interviewees appears in Appendix H.[1] The responses received to the questionnaire have been compiled in Tables 17-A to 17-G.

Motivational Urges and General Outlook

This was enquired by questions 1 to 9. The picture we got can somewhat be described as follows:

(a) most of the industry people (executives and top management level) feel happy and satisfied in spite of their various problems. They are in business and as entrepreneurs they probably enjoy it as a vehicle of satisfaction and earning and take problems in their stride. Most people feel that the industry is growing and has bright future though there is also a perceptible concern with some that the direction of growth is not towards moral and healthy lines. They feel that the industry should keep up with the technological developments and maintain the growth it has already achieved, work towards upliftment of Indian culture and development of artists along with encouraging new and upcoming ones, work for education and cross-cultural understanding, even though earning is an important, and for some the most important, motive. Eradication of piracy is important but is not usually seen as the primary goal.

(b) about the industry's own role, the respondents feel that they have a significant role to play. While entertainment is important for some, cross-cultural appreciation is an important contribution which the phonograms can make. As they see it, the goals are development of artistic values and education and many feel that they have to be responsive to the people's needs. Some also see their goal as cultural creation. Most of them are optimistic about the phonogram industry inspite of the problems which may be seen more as challenges rather than discouraging factors.

Comments: We are inclined to deduce a general conclusion that while some constructive, creative and unconventional thinking is present, especially among some new emerging entrepreneurs, it is more than evident that a major motivation is earning and commercial profits. This is quite understandable and there is nothing reprehensible about this but what is not appreciated is that not only some nobler and moral values but also other social and cultural functions of the industry become subservient to the monetary motive.

Two examples may be cited here: the industry's role in not working for, and their indifference to, preserving the cultural heritage, though it was easily within their means to do so, has been decried by several writers (Danielou, 1952; Raghavan, 1953; Kunst, 1959).[2] As for their dubious role many artists and others have felt that the industry also contributes to the piracy problem, indirectly by some of their policies and directly by unscrupulous means. There are evidences — they may be casual but they certainly point to the existing malady — that the music of one industry is pirated by another and in one case it was a multinational who allegedly did so. It is also possible that industries indulge in this malpractice through some other labels or through some associates. There are also evidences that artists felt 'cheated'. I may quote one artist: 'I am not ready to go for recording again to . . . They have cheated me.'

Recording Industry and the Government

Questions 10, 11 and 12 dealt with this. Table 17-B lists the areas of concern. Most of the respondents felt that there was a general lack of awareness of industry's problems by the government, and also about the role of phonograms as a cultural medium. They suggested immediate check on piracy. Many responded that they were not satisfied with government's role though some positive reactions also emerged. Many felt that the government did not have a cultural policy and suggested exemption of various taxes and removal of excise which will result in the promotion of this important cultural medium.

Comments: Interviews with several persons give us an impression that import policy needs to be reviewed. There is dearth of quality raw material, especially audio-magnetic tapes. As these are not allowed they are brought either by smuggling or as personal baggage which make these items much costlier than direct imports. It was suggested that these materials may be treated as cultural materials at par with books, or movie films and if restrictions are removed or at least relaxed, it will not only make materials cheap and of good quality but, by reducing the price, will help in a larger consumption.[3]

The excise and taxation policy comes in for attack in the interviews also in many other ways. This contributes in making these products costly. While the excise is either exempted or reduced on blank cassettes, records are still subject to excise which make them more expensive and this naturally tilts the consumer in favour of tapes. Moreover, the record-playing instruments also become expensive due to various governmental costs which are levied as imposts. In addition, the sales tax, along with other local and state taxes, add to the ultimate costs. It may be said for the government that in many cases it cannot take abrupt decisions even when it is aware of the problems. The sales tax is such a case. Its abolition is already within the government's consideration for a long time but as this is a state subject, a decision cannot be taken without a consensus and this is the most difficult block in arriving at a decision.

Relationship with the Artists, Producers and others

Questions 13 to 18 attempted to obtain the industry's views on this subject. The general picture can be described as under:

Most of the industry's personnel felt that artists were satisfied with them and the major reasons for such satisfaction, as they saw it, were either (a) good and prompt royalty payments, or (b) the cordiality in personal and business relationship, but they also felt that there was a scope for improvement. Most respondents felt that there should be an uniform royalty payment system though it may also differ or be negotiable. About the need for changing the present policy of exclusive contract, the sample was equally divided; hence, no clear indication was evident. There are varying responses about the period and type of contract and about proper monitoring.

Comments: This is a crucial relationship which concerns both the involved parties and it is but obvious that they will have a different perceptions of each other. Both have different motivations and expectations and even though they may be similar, the order of priority and the intensity of each may differ. It is not surprising, therefore, that most (industry) respondents stated their (subjective) opinion that artists were, more or less, satisfied with them. In this connection, we may refer to a study in Europe (Blaukopf, 1985) which asked the industry what chances they offered to creative artists, an area of utmost concern to all artists for their job-satisfaction. Most respondents answered that they gave ample opportunities, but according to Blaukopf, 'experience has shown that there is a tension between the necessarily subjective approach of the creative artist on the one hand and the rational realism required for the fulfilment of the management tasks on the other'. This expectance-discrepancy obviously requires a good handling of interpersonal relationship. A satisfactory relationship here will result in the growth for both as both are dependent on each other. The feelings of trust and cordiality must be maintained and it is good to see that quite a number of emerging entrepreneurs keep artists' welfare and satisfaction in their active consideration, as one top emerging entrepreneur stated: 'If we eat, our bread is earned through the artist, . . . we get ideas for recording from the artists'.

Questions 13 to 18 were related to this area and Table 17-D shows the responses received. Artists, except the big ones, are seldom accorded the respect and treatment they deserve. They are more considered as, 'trade items', rather than living resources. According to an interviewee, 'artists are treated like "bonded labourers (serfs)" by the big companies.' They are not paid royalty properly and not given proper chances; yet, when they sing for other companies, the companies object to the release of their cassettes. According to some, (an example was cited above) the artists are 'cheated' by these companies – the main defaults being in compensation payment, exclusive contracting, and jumping of royalty if not properly monitored.

There seems to be an awareness now that satisfied artists are companies' big assets. This also is probably the prime motive for the recent MRTP (Monopolies and Restrictive Trade Practices) Commission which has put the maximum period of contract as 3 years[4] except in cases of new artists where it can be extended to 5 years. However, artists still feel restrained and want to have the freedom to sing and contract. Some artists suggested an artists' union to protect their interests.

An awareness is now appearing in artists to assert themselves to prevent such exploitation by organised companies. Besides some clamouring for unions, artists are now joining to run their own enterprises. An instance is 'KUSSADIG' a joint concern started by some artists themselves, a break-away group from the GRAMCO. The KAPCO International is owned by a graduate from the Film and TV Institute, Pune and in a short period – it was commissioned in 1983 – it has given an impressive record.[5]

Copyright

Questions 19 to 23 sought responses to these matters. The responses are shown in Table 17-E. The broad picture we get is that most producers felt that in the Copyright Act, 1984 Amendment some clauses (which are aimed at curbing piracy) are neither effective nor effectively implemented. The major reasons for non-implementation are lack of publicity, impracticability, involving time-consuming and costly legal processes and lack of governmental understanding. The government can help, they think, by giving more powers to producers, artists and authorities and the check on piracy can be more effective if checks are made at the sources or shops which sell such goods. The industry itself can play a better and more effective role in this matter of copyright problems if there is more cooperation and coordination which, perhaps, is lacking now. Some suggested that there should be an umbrella union where each producer is represented.

Comments: All legislations presuppose, for success, an effective implementation and cooperation from all concerned people. They, by themselves, cannot solve all problems. In this light, the piracy cannot be curbed — as far as this is one of the aims of the Copyright — unless there is a support from all those who are affected by this evil. As already stated earlier, some established companies themselves indulge in jumping copyrights and pirating products which are not their own, exchanging and selling copyrights of the master tapes and other malpractices. This leads to corruption and bribery and thus obstructs a successful implementation and the vicious circle continues. While we expect the government to deliver goods, the industry and other involved people, the artists, and consumers included have also to be prudent.

The purpose of the Copyright regulations is to protect the interest of the artists/performers and the industries and to prevent any anti-social application, so that all get their due share. For curbing the piracy, the 1984 Amendment to the Copyright law prescribes strict penalties and deterrent punishment but how far it succeeds may depend upon its proper implementation and other factors. Hemant Kumar (Kumar, 1985) doubts if the present Amendment by itself would make much of a difference to the situation. According to him, one way to fight is to reduce the tax burden and eliminate the price differential between a regular cassette and a pirated one; at present, the pirated cassettes are Rs. 10 to Rs. 15 cheaper than the regular ones.

It is unfortunate that Copyright protection is solely seen as aimed towards curbing piracy — at least as we gather from the responses or from the interviews, this seem to be the most important concern. Nowhere, there was any reference to the broader implication of human rights protection in the spirit of UNESCO or the Universal Copyright Convention. The latter refers to the three rights — Rights of (i) authors, (ii) performers, and (iii) producers of phonograms (UNESCO, 1984). This reflects a narrow self-preservation attitude which is not conducive to the all-round development of this industry or its product – the phonogram. Attitudes and major concerns, as we all know, affect the corresponding behaviour and performance.

Import-Export

Questions 24 to 29 dealt with this area. Table 17-E shows the responses. The questions were answered by only one respondent possibly because not many are engaged in this line. The principal concern of this one respondent organisation was the non-availability of quality tapes through government. It suggested easy import and speedy export without much formalities and felt that the popularity of Indian music abroad was more because of cultural reasons though economic and political factors also are quite important. He felt that the interest in Indian music is growing in foreign countries.

Comments: I think it is almost universally felt that exports are highly encouraged and there are several incentives. The export of phonograms would be, so we think, highly welcome as it is not only a trade proposition but it helps dissemination of Indian cultural material and results in more cross-cultural appreciation. However, it is also universally felt that the procedures are too heavy; there is laborious paper-work and it takes time so that 'it would seem that government does not want a company to export', that 'it was a tedious task', and was 'no incentive at all'. As for the imports, there is an awareness for the need of more cassettes; it is, however, projected that there would be more internal production and this would reduce the imports.[6, 7]

Problems Facing the Industry

The most important problem perceived by the industry, as coming again and again in our discussions, is PIRACY – responded so by all. Other problems were (i) non-availability, and (ii) paucity of quality tapes. They also felt that the general public was not aware of their problems and suggested a more strict governmental policy for speedy punishment of pirates, quality control in tape-production and proper implementation and relaxation of rigid procedures.

Comments: On basis of interviews, we see the major problems as follows:

(i) the first and most important, of course, is *piracy*. The pirated cassettes are widely sold and freely available almost everywhere though there are some pockets where this business is more hectic.[8] An industry personnel said, characteristically, that by the time this study was published, probably the industry would not be existing! This is certainly an exaggeration but it indicates the gravity of the problem. According to usually reliable sources, only about 5 per cent is the legal business — the rest is controlled by pirates. Industry is obviously concerned about this; it has been reflected in the abrupt dropping of sales during early eighties, though it is now picking up. A study by Kuckreja (1984) has reported the colossal loss to the industry, the government and the artists, due to piracy.[9] Hemant Kumar, cited above, has termed this piracy business as, 'highly organised, endemic'. According to him, an 'artist is losing anything like one to one-and-a-half lakhs of rupees every six months in terms of royalties.' (of course, he is speaking of 'class one' artists but we can also guess the plight of smaller ones, though they have less chances of being pirated.)

The other important problems are the same as expressed in the responses:

(ii) heavy taxation which pushes the prices of the products, and
(iii) non-availability of quality tapes.

While the government can certainly help in this matter by appropriate legislations, implementation and policies, industries themselves must take the initiative in solving some of these problems. A strong resistance to all sub-standard materials, a quality consciousness, a monitoring of their own practices, and a strong cooperative effort will go a long way to check piracy and improve matters. Perhaps this is what many interviewees meant when they stated that a cooperation and coordination within industries themselves is needed.[10]

Three questions - 30, 31 and 32 - deal with this area; Table 17-F lists the responses received.

Future of Recording Industry

Questions 33 and 34 asked the industry's opinion about the future and the challenges. Table 17-G lists the responses. Most people – all respondents – felt that the future of the industry was bright and promising. The challenges before them of piracy and other problems are real but what is, perhaps, more important is the need for keeping abreast of and coping with new developments in technology.

Comments: The above optimism is shared by persons who were interviewed. All were hopeful about the prospects of this industry because the music industry, which is now becoming an entertainment and leisure industry, will continue to grow as the public will always like to hear music – of course what they would like to hear and how, would change with the times. The business can cash on this public demand – the only pre-requisite is to adapt the style of working, the fare to be presented, and the technology to the needs. However, all were not so optimistic about the record industry *vis-a-vis* the tapes though hopes were expressed due to the inherent qualitative superiority of records, as also their appeal to more sensitive ears. According to some, the records should be encouraged because they are, perhaps, the best safeguard against piracy – they are difficult to reproduce — while, according to some, the largest consumers of records are the pirates!

Emergence of 2 non-IPI record pressing organisations – the Oriental and the Jyoti, both at Bombay – is an enough evidence that the record business is not so bad as it looks or as it is presented, but holds sufficient promise. The recent establishment of yet another Record manufacturing unit, the Kapco International at Delhi (with factory in Himachal Pradesh) is another sign of the growing popularity, demand and prospects. Kapco has been doing record pressing for several other organisation besides doing their own work and has done quite well. This shows that the future of the record industry in particular and of phonogram in general is bright. No doubt, there are problems, some of them quite severe, but these are the challenges of the business.

Status of the Artists

Questionnaire 3 attempts to probe this. After asking his or her professional status and other informatory details, the artist was asked to mark 20 carefully selected statements along a 5-point scale extending from 'Strongly Agree (SA)' to 'Strongly Disagree (SD)'. The statements were drawn from the major concerns shown by the artists during pilot interviews regarding the royalty, contracts and their perception of the relationship with the industry as a whole. This is not an attitude scale as such as it has not undergone the psychometric refinements necessary for such scaling, but it is a step towards making one by pin-pointing some special areas of concern and experience and is an attempt to develop criterial referents and items on that basis.

This questionnaire was responded to by only 11 artists — singers and instrumentalists — all through personal interviews. It is too small a sample and that, too, not a representative one but selected only on the basis of convenience and availability. We, however, tried to take some from North (Delhi: only one who was also separately interviewed) and some from South (Madras and Bangalore). The responses do indicate a trend, the concerns and the way they look at the things, though we may not generalise at this stage.

Table 18 shows these items and the frequency of responses distributed among the 5 points. We have also shown the frequencies of the two extremes combined to read it as a 3-point scale, if necessary, which would indicate probably a more reliable trend of responses because a 5-point scale demands a finer discrimination which is not always possible unless the questionnaire is well-prepared and interviews well-designed.

The responses which we have received can be grouped in three categories:

(i) areas of maximum agreement,
(ii) areas of mild agreement, and
(iii) areas of uncertainty, minimum or no agreement.

As we see this, these are as follows:

Areas of Maximum Agreement:

(a) Artists should be free to sing for any company they like (item 6),
(b) Artists share equal responsibility . . . in fighting against piracy and other unauthorised reproduction of recorded programmes (item 20),
(c) Artists should have an association of their own (item 16),
(d) Recording companies should also go for new and talented

artists rather than make use of only established ones, which in other words means that the recording companies do not make much use of the available talent (item 3),

(e) Industry realises that a phonogram is a cultural instrument and this is almost universally felt by all (item 1). How far this assessment is true, however, needs further examination for we have already seen in analysis of questionnaire 2 that not all industry people think of phonogram as an instrument of cultural development,

(f) Companies do not have much concern about the welfare of the artists (item 10),

(g) There is much to be desired as far as royalty payments are concerned (item 12), and that royalty payments may not be made conditional upon signing of an exclusive contract (item 7),

(h) However, the artists-respondents do not think that the existing 'cassette boom' has adversely affected the people's interest in live performances (item 17).

Areas of Mild Agreement

(a) Concern for royalty and compensation system (items 14 and 15). More people think that an uniform royalty rate is preferable to other modes of payment and that flat payments for each programme are better than royalty payments,

(b) Existing contract system (item 7): artists feel that royalty payment should be detached from an exclusive contract system,

(c) Disappointment of the artists with the organised companies who, according to them, do not fully meet their expectations (item 19).

Areas of Minimum or no Agreement or of Uncertainty

(a) The feeling of disappointment with organised industries is also reflected in the sizable responses to item 18: there should be less number of recording companies doing more organised business than more companies doing less organised business. An equal number, however, seems to think otherwise, probably because the unorganised sector gives or promises better returns and is (seen as) a check on the monopoly of organised business.

(b) Relationship expected from record companies (item 8): More persons felt that the record companies maintained good relations though an almost equal number was not so certain about this.

(c) Elimination of exclusive contract system (item 5): More people felt that it should be discontinued though an equal number was uncertain about this; however, none was for continuation of this system.

(d) Method of promoting young artists (item 4): opinions were equally divided as to whether this financial risk be taken or not; half of respondents thought this should be done even at some financial risk while the other half thought it should be done with discretion.

(e) Artists seem to be unsure whether the compensation given was reasonable or not (item 13).

(f) Artists also felt uncertain whether the royalty rates should be the same for all type of artists irrespective of their popularity and prestige (item 14).

In brief, an overall analysis of these responses, to the extent they reflect the opinion of a wider sample, indicate that a majority of artists feel,

(i) that the companies do not encourage new talents, do not care much about their welfare, and are not primarily motivated by cultural considerations,

(ii) that the exclusive contract system needs to be revised or changed along with the royalty terms,

(iii) that they feel strongly about their own existence and identity as a group and their professional freedom, and do not appreciate the constraints placed on them by the companies, and

(iv) they are aware of the importance of the cultural role of the industry and they realise that they also share the responsibility in making it worthwhile, in checking piracy and establishment of healthy norms.

We now conclude our analysis of the data received through the three questionnaires, interviews and other documental sources. It may be explained that while we have tried to classify the data in several categories, the responses highly overlap. This is especially true of Questionnaire 2 where the intermixing of categories is highly visible. The categories are not mutually exclusive – thus, a response in Import-export is also a likely response in Problems and Relationship with Government or a response about the Relationship with Artists also a possible response in Copyright etc. Our analysis also shows this overlap and occasional repetition, as each category has been dealt separately. In Questionnaire 3 also such overlap is evident.

In Questionnaire 3, our basis for classifying responses in areas of (i) maximum, (ii) minimum, or (iii) uncertain agreement has broadly been the consideration of the number of Agreement points in excess of others (neutral or disagreement). It must be admitted, however, that this might also reflect a subjective assessment or a personal bias after seeing the distribution. A wider sample with more thoroughly planned instruments and an item analysis will, naturally, reduce this personal factor.

NOTES

1. Persons interviewed are not identified for reasons of confidentiality.
2. See note 3 of Chapter 1, for excerpts from Raghavan, and Kunst. According to Danielou (quoted by Kunst), 'if the sales of a record fail to reach a certain figure during a three-monthly period, the record is automatically destroyed. . . . Almost all the records of musicians of the past generation have been destroyed.'
   The methods, and the time-lag might have changed in this long period but, possibly, the attitude remains the same as it was in 1952.
3. See responses to Questionnaire 2, Table 17. Some opinions and suggestions are:
   — import policy needs to be reviewed
   — import of raw materials may be permitted, especially of tapes; cassettes imported directly will be much cheaper than if smuggled or imported as personal baggage, or as unauthorised imports.
   — import of these cultural materials may be treated at par with import of books etc. Like cinematographic films, special licenses may be allowed.
4. As referred by Basu (1985) in the box, 'Minor Skirmishes' on page 21, of 'Update'. According to some, the maximum period is one year now; this is, however, not verified, and also possibly not a fact. Before this regulation came in force in 1974, recording companies (the HMV primarily) could direct their dealers to stock only their products to the exclusion of any other (Polydor; for

only it existed at that time). Since early 1974, under new norms, all dealers could stock records from all companies.

5. See note 2 of Chapter 3; Mr Rajinder Gandhi of Kalyani Recording Co., was a lecturer at the Film and TV Institute, Pune, and has vast experience in the field of recording.
6. See note 12 of Chapter 1.
7. The following information is from Kuckreja (1984): Indian exports go all over the world, the principal markets being UK; USA; East European countries; the Middle-East; the West Indies; East Africa; Malaysia; Singapore and Fiji. Despite severe handicaps (of rampant piracy and fierce competition) export of records grew at a fast rate from less than Rs. 64 lakh in July 1972/June 1973 to over Rs. 2.10 crores in July 1977/June 1978, an increase of 229 per cent in 6 years! The main reason was the increasing awareness and interest in Indian Classical and Folk music, in all major countries of the world. The records manufacturers also export western music records to East European countries despite fierce competition from local and overseas manufacturers.
   In fact, HMV has received the top exports award from the PLEX COUNCIL for five consecutive years: 1973-74 to 1977-78.
8. In Lajpatrai Market centre of Delhi — a pocket where this trade is mostly concentrated — it is estimated that there are about 500 shops dealing in cassettes, about 90 per cent of them fake ones. One could easily guess the size of trade taking in account several pockets in Delhi (though probably not all as big as the one mentioned above), and large cities in India, besides the other 3 metropolitan cities — Madras, Bombay and Calcutta — all thriving seaports and much larger than Delhi.
9. Kuckreja bases his figures on the conservative estimates formulated by the IPI for the year 1982: a sale of 3 crore cassettes (both legitimate and pirated), where the share of pirated cassettes is estimated at 90 per cent:

   1. Loss to the govt. due to evasion of taxes - 41 per cent - on Rs. 20.00 a cassette ... Rs. 15.58 crore
   2. Loss to artists, producers and other copyright owners @ $12\frac{1}{2}$% ... Rs. 6.00 crore
   3. Total loss ... Rs. 21.58 crore

   A crore is 10 million; Loss to Income-tax is yet extra.
   Excise duty was raised from 8 per cent to 26.25 per cent in 1982 budget; thus, the over-all price differential (gain to pirates) was Rs. 10.00 per cassette - Rs. 5.50 on account of saving the taxes, and Rs. 4.50 on account of royalty and artwork. (Basu, 1985).
10. According to an interviewee, the industry can check the piracy by lowering the prices; in fact, recent lowering of prices had visible effect. 'This is what the industry can do to beat the pirates. People want good quality at low price. If the industry cannot meet this demand, they will go to the pirate. It is inevitable.'

5

CONCLUSIONS AND SUGGESTIONS FOR FURTHER RESEARCH

WE HAVE now come to the end of our study. We have discussed how the industry developed in India, and that it was no mere accident that it came but was a logical development of a process of inter-cultural change and people's readiness to accept new changes. We also discussed how the industry which came more as an instrument of exploitation of Indian people for a commercial interest established itself and endeared itself so that this also caused vast cultural changes, made hitherto private cultural matters accessible to common people and helped inter-cultural dissemination and diffusion. We also discussed how the industry has passed and is still passing through various vicissitudes and how it is becoming responsive to people's needs bringing in its wake various problems and expansion strategies, piracy and immense growth of regional and some national organisations to threaten the monopoly of the established traditional business. Lastly, we discussed our own study which aimed at knowing from various sources and the data collected from industries, artists and others what actually is the status of the industry at present – its future development promises, its potential, its problems and its direction of growth.

It is now time for us to coordinate all these findings which we have discussed and see in light of our original plan how they are relevant to and can be related to our initial objectives, which in essence are to consider how the information we have gathered can lead us to examine (i) the role of phonograms in cultural development, (ii) the phonograms as determinants and also the consequences of socio-cultural changes, and (iii) the phonographic industry as a part of this entire network – culture, cultural behaviour, cultural music-makers and culture (music) consumers. We must also discuss here the important concerns of industry such as piracy, which not only threatens the regular and legitimate industry but which may lead to an unsocial and lopsided development. We will also discuss some concerns of the artists as they are the cog-wheels on which the industry runs. Lastly, we may also discuss some important questions which may be answered and some significant areas that have emerged and require a further study or research, or just a survey. In this, our criteria are mainly three:

(i) that technology must serve mankind,
(ii) it must have implications for proper socio-cultural planning, and
(iii) that it should not be an instrument to further the vested interest of some at the cost of many.

What we see today, unfortunately, is that there is a fast and mad race for supremacy even in this humane area of cultural technology in which the man – the most important element – is mostly forgotten and is the one at the receiving end. He is still important but not as a creator or the active element or an initiator but as a passive object on which to test new theories – mostly pre-determined – and development strategies. It is not the man who must change for the sake of technology and conditions should be created for bringing necessary changes in technology to suit the technology user, not *vice versa*.

As it is not possible to discuss all these issues at length here, we will limit our discussion to (i) trend, (ii) concerns, and (iii) suggestions for further research. In-between, however, we will have occasions to deal with matters which may have implications for issues raised.

Trends

In spite of the severe limitations in coverage and the nature of data as explained elsewhere, it is possible to reach certain broad conclusions on the basis of the information received. We presume that the 22 organisations we have covered give us enough comparable data which can be projected to the entire industry as a whole. Though we did not receive information from all the IPI members, we also perhaps left a good number of non-IPI organisations some of which are of a substantial size, such as the T-series, which, we understand, controls about 80 to 90 per cent of the pre-recorded cassette market, especially in film music. As regards Releases, Production and Sale, we find that film music still predominates – though now the pre-recorded cassettes are outnumbering records.

This is true of the reported figures but when we consider the vast spurious production and unreported releases – the picture becomes quite glaring. Because of the emergence of several companies in recent years the market value of the traditional labels have come down especially as the current mass production is the pre-recorded cassette whose recording methods are relatively simpler and less subject to quality variations. 'New companies are (also) giving good service', as one artist commented. There is also an emergence of regional music and various types of musical category are being tapped – a company either specialising in one or more categories or catering to specific regions, communities or languages. There seems to be a ready market for different types of music but one must take risks, experiment and evolve suitable market strategies.

It seems that except for film music where cassettes rule supreme, discs are still regarded as important recording medium – first, because the quality of their reproduction is far superior to that of cassettes; secondly, some feel that cassettes do not last as much as records do and production of records is one way to curb piracy, as records are more difficult to duplicate than cassettes; and thirdly, as the records are more lasting they are better suited for the traditional music which one wants to preserve. This trend of the revival of records and their promise is evident in the fact that many new organisations which started with cassette production have also taken to the record production perhaps to cater to a more sensitive and quality-conscious market.

This also indicates the promise of records for some selected music-categories, especially of low usage while the cassettes will probably continue to cater to the mass market. One retarding factor in record production is the high cost of recording and also of the player instruments, especially the electronic stereo equipments which are currently in vogue. As for the production, record pressing companies are not many and until recently it was only one (GRAMCO) which still is the largest, but now, the minimum orders they accept is from 500 to 750 pressings whereas it was around 200 pressings about a decade ago. This has escalated the cost and many people find it easier to produce cassettes rather than to lock up money in an unstable market. However, the existence of 6 recording companies now – 3 multi-nationals and 3 Indian companies, of which 2 came in existence during the seventies, one about 2 years ago and the most recent one only about 6 months ago – indicates the reviving trend of increasing record potential.

Market Strategies

The emergence of new industries, outside the so far traditional IPI monopoly, has brought in a variety of marketing strategies. The new organisations cover a wide spectrum of structure, ownership and size and this naturally leads to a neck-to-neck competition for survival and supremacy. The market strategies are no more dictated by monopoly organisations and traditional codes; they are more dictated by a spirit of competition and bargaining between the parties involved – performers and producers, and organisations with a view to the consumer market.

A glaring instance is the contract system. While, so far, it was only the exclusive contract system on royalty basis – and which still holds as the general rule of operation – the contractual arrangements are now often dictated by organisational bargaining. This has resulted in a variety of contracts: spot payment, flat payment, one-time contract, exclusive contract but differing in periods etc. This new realisation of performers' role is evident in the MRTP (Monopolies and Restrictive Trade Practices) Commission's code that the maximum period of exclusive contract will be 3 years though it has conceded 5 years in case of new artists. The MRTP Commission has also stipulated that all retail outlets can now stock all types of records and cassettes from all producers, rather than tied to one only, as was the case before the new regulations came in force. This shows the penetration of performers/artists/producers in regulating marketing and contractual practices. Response to the consumer interests – the third element in the communication system after the music makers and industry – is not yet forcefully evident except that new types of music are being introduced to cater to a new market which was hitherto unexplored or only was minimally tapped. However, it seems it is a matter of time only when the consumer will also be a strong force to reckon with in the modelling of marketing and production strategies of the industry and the cultural policy of the government.

Consumer Behaviour

An examination of the changing consumer interests and the data in various tables indicate that,

(i) film music still dominates – it will continue to dominate because of various reasons such as (a) its appeal to people at all social and cultural levels, (b) its continuing search for new styles and compositions, and (c) its responsiveness to the people's need for melody and light music. An important fourth factor is that it is fast becoming a source of new music and new musical experiments. Music has always been an integral part of films in India and many old songs have become part of our national heritage due to their wizardry, purity, composition and melody. In fact, this area of film and music is so vast that it requires a separate study by itself for any meaningful comprehension of this phenomenon.

To come back to our point, the film music will continue to dominate the Indian sound recording scene. It is also becoming very popular abroad. The major changes which are coming now are (i) that this music is now distributed among various organisations while it was monopolised by only one up to only a decade ago, (ii) that it is becoming a music for mass consumption and is available more on tapes, than on records, which makes it cheaper to possess and enjoy, and (iii) that the piracy is maximum in this category.

(ii) Another type of music which is fast coming up is the devotional. Devotional music has a perennial appeal for Indian masses though it is apparent that film songs and the new music are now 'polluting' the serenity and purity of this music. Some of the recent singers, however, are rendering the classic and pure lyrics into new tunes and these are becoming popular.

(iii) After devotional, it is the regional music of different varieties that is now coming up. All regions of India are rich in musical varieties, including folk music and while some have been in the field for a long time (such as Bengal), many are now getting new openings.

Concerns

If the phonogram as a cultural communication intervention and the industry as the supplier and user of technology and software have to play their cherished roles, we must refer to some common areas of concern to those involved – artists, industry and the government, and, also, the consumer. Of course, each of these elements share different reasons for concern but the total effect is the retardation of the entire system which hampers its full development. We will discuss here some major concerns of the industry and the artists, the two most important elements of this system.

Piracy

The first and the foremost concern is the piracy which affects both – industry as well as artists – and results in severe losses for the government and, as far as the consumer is concerned, it mostly offers them a sub-standard material, though at a cheaper price. According to the IFPI brochure of 1983, 95 per cent of the total spurious production is controlled by pirates, another 5 per cent by counterfeiters, and India is a region of over 80 per cent pirate market of over 80 per cent of the total sales. However, the incidence of piracy has been estimated even more: up to about 95 per cent or even more according to various sources; in fact, a senior industry personnel felt, the industry would not exist by the time this report was published. This is probably an exaggeration for otherwise nobody would invest so much developmental capital in a sinking market and most would have been preparing to wind up rather than find ways and means to remain in the market and prosper, but it is certainly true that this is an important area of concern to all involved.

There are several reasons for this amount of piracy. While the human nature and greed is partly responsible, the indirect contribution of the existing establishments is not much less. Let us elaborate on some of these reasons:

(i) The organised companies themselves are responsible considerably as they exploited the masses by the high prices of their products due to the monopoly they enjoyed and "made hay while the sun shone." Asks the '*Eye Spy*'[1]: 'Are they themselves not responsible for much of the piracy when they grossly overpriced the cassettes they were selling? Otherwise, how could they bring down the price by almost 50 per cent?' Even now, there are two chief types of regular cassettes: the film cassettes which are most copied have been almost halved (though the prices of spurious cassettes are still lower) while the not-so vulnerable recording such as of the copyrighted masters etc. are sold at high rates but the sale is not much affected because perhaps they are not available in spurious market, have better sound quality, have better tapes, and have a selected audience. The establishments were also not responsive to the market needs but manipulated production and sales to fit their own commercial schemes. They also exploited the artists who, once they entered the exclusive contract, were at their mercy; it was at least hypothetically possible – we do not know to what extent this was actually practised but have reasons to believe that this was not an unknown practice and it was within their power – to make or unmake an artist by giving or not giving them the required recording and publicity. Some instances of how some great artists were handled by such organisations are cited by Joshi (1984) who was a recording executive with the HMV (His Master's Voice – GRAMCO) for several years,[2] and one artist in an interview stated that he would never go to a particular company. Such isolated instances as the last one do not enable us to make any generalisation but they certainly point to a malady – somewhere the relationship turns sour. These sources of dissatisfaction, some direct like charging high prices due to a monopoly, and some indirect like the alienation of artists, do all create a breeding ground on which the pirates thrive.

(ii) *Market needs*: This was already mentioned above but requires further elaboration. Success in all consumer industries presupposes a sensitiveness to market needs and development of an appropriate marketing strategy so that not only the products reflect the need of the market, but also reach where they are needed. In a large and multi-cultural country like India this requires a special effort and one must work for exploring new areas of expansion. The almost monopoly of a few organisations in the past perhaps led to a certain complacency as there was already an established market and a target audience. It is but natural that a void created by a discrepancy between the market needs and their fulfilment by the companies must be filled in and, if the established organisations fail to cope with this, new entrepreneurs will come. We may call this spoiling the market or undercutting, but this is partly the creation of the existing environment.

A good sensitivity to the market needs also presupposes a constant search for new sources and research on consumer interests and behaviour. The monopoly concerns were, perhaps slow, and as they did well in a sellers' market there was no pressing need to tap new sources or to introduce new lines except when it served their own purpose. There are certainly several exceptions but reasons for this neglect are not far to seek. Increasing cost of production necessitates working on projects which promise a good return. The established set of procedures also come into the way of development. Here the role of an entrepreneur is clearly visible: an entrepreneur is not bothered by the conventional rules which he would circumvent or change as far as possible within the circumstances and he is flexible enough as his major intention is to penetrate an established market.[3]

(iii) *Human nature:* This is an important reason which, if not regulated by internal or external disciplines, results in the lack of social responsibility and proper norms of social conduct. Every activity or undertaking carries with it some social responsibility – a consciousness for its implications for the society and for the people who are involved. Most people, we presume, have this sense but the threshold where this control ends and the motive for individual gain at the cost of social consciousness comes up, differs in different individuals and societies. This sense is somewhat kept afloat by suitable laws, codes of social conduct and social norms but they also incite the opposite motive especially if such codes are contrary to one's basic motive or disposition. In our case, as an instance, if the basic motive is earning, stiff taxation policy or anything which hampers it, may be resented and may give rise to abnormal and unsocial conduct. This is reinforced by the lack of implementation and by a feeling that the consequences could somehow be evaded.

The tendency for indulgence in anti-social conducts is very difficult to check without a concerted effort on the part of all involved – artists, government, consumers and, perhaps, the industries themselves. Interviews with representatives of artists and industry show that both are conscious of their role in coping not only with this malpractice of piracy in particular but also others which pollute the social, cultural or economic environment.[4] All of them in one way or another contribute to this malpractice – we are chiefly concerned here with piracy – and the feeling of getting away from the consequences – social, legal or otherwise. Any kind of legislation will only be a patchwork because this matter concerns deeper motives and any exterior but unacceptable controls would only give rise to defensive reactions and effort to circumvent the controls.[5] One way of preventing this is an open multi-party dialogue along with the representatives of pirates in a non-threatening environment so that all can frankly discuss their reservations, realise their part in the entire operation, may give vent to their feelings, can reach a joint solution and feel responsible for its implementation.

Copyright

This is another important concern of the industry. However, this is much related to the piracy problem and much of what was stated above is relevant here also.

Another important concern of the industry which emerges is the high cost of the quality blank tapes, their non-availability and importing difficulties. The issue is further aggravated by the high excise in addition to already high local and state taxes. We understand that excise duty has recently been abolished on blank tapes for small-scale manufacturers but is still there for large-scale producers and on records, making the latter a costlier production. If the phonograms have to play their role in cultural communication system, all such problems which affect the quality, price and production should be openly discussed and solved. It was a general opinion that the tapes and records be considered as cultural materials and hence may be provided the facilities given to such materials.[6] Moreover, the differential taxation is, perhaps, leading to another malpractice – large companies manufacturing under different labels or in the name of smaller (but associated) concerns tending either to avoid the taxation altogether or to have benefit of reduced taxation.

Two areas which mostly concern the artists are *royalty* and *con-*

tracts. Let us take the royalty first. Not only the royalty payments vary[7] for different recording companies and for different artists according to their status (or marketability?) but also the royalties are not paid regularly. This is more deplorable as some of the well-known companies, including some multi-nationals, are involved. Sometimes, huge arrears are involved. A recent report[8] refers to a suit filed by a film-maker against a multi-national company for recovery of substantial royalty arrears against the sale of records of a film. While this isolated instance, which is still to be adjudged and is being contested does not enable us to make any generalisation, the majority of artists who were interviewed showed concern about this.[9] For one affluent person of the status of a film-producer who goes to the court to claim their dues, there may be several individuals and poor artists who do not have the resources nor time to do so.

Artists have not only expressed concern about royalty, they have suggested that a rethinking may be needed to relax the rigidity about the terms of royalty payment which are now highly loaded for the companies. They also suggest rethinking about terms of contract so that they give to the artists a sense of freedom. As it is, the present system of exclusive contracts and other terms make him feel almost like a 'bonded labourer (serf)' entirely at the mercy of the company. It is true that this system offers a security so necessary for a budding artist, but this certainly does not satisfy his creative talents and he feels stifled.

It is for this reason that the artists feel they are used more as instruments and are nothing more than mere items of trade and some of them suggested formation of a fraternity, an association or a union to protect their interests. As we understand from various interviews, there is unfortunately no such association in Delhi though perhaps one exists in Bombay.[10]

Suggestions for Further Research

Following are some significant areas where further studies can be useful. It is obvious that this vast area of the role of phonograms in cultural communication, their impact on socio-cultural system as also the determination of technology by the changing consumer behaviour, carries within itself an immense scope for further investigations. The areas presented here only illustrate these possibilities:

1. This study itself was done under several constraints – of time and coverage, as was described in an earlier chapter. However, it was a satisfying effort in that it opened up a vast arena which was not systematically studied earlier, to the best knowledge of the writer. It may be worthwhile to follow-up this study on a larger sample, with better experimental design, supplemented by carefully constructed instruments, interviews and covering a wider region. It is expected that this will give us a wider perspective from which to appreciate the role of this technological development in Indian life. Inasmuch as India is one of the highly multi-cultural, ancient and developed society among the developing nations of the so-called third world, such a study would not only be socially relevant but will also point to various factors which operated during cultural changes within the country due to external impacts.
2. A significant area which emerges is the possibility of a study of the status of the artists in its various aspects: his or her relationship with the recording companies, evaluation of his role and status, and the process and extent of self-actualisation of his role as an active component of the culture and communication system rather than a passive 'item of the trade'. Self-actualization includes, among others, the maximum development of one's skills and creative abilities along with a sense of self-fulfilment and satisfaction. In this, we may have also to consider how much active party he is in several contractual considerations. For instance, a mass consumer of phonograms, the All India Radio or Akashvani, have a contractual arrangement only with the recording companies who are paid the fixed royalty.[11] We do not yet know what part of this goes to the artists because, for every record sold (on which perhaps the royalty is paid), there are, perhaps, other multi-reproductions permitted in the contract between the company and the consumer but where the artist does not have any say or share. For a welfare society who wants to give every person his due, provisions which show a concern for the artists should be a part of the contract, and not that this becomes a purely commercial contract between two parties.
3. An area of utmost significance which deserves attention is that of film music, where the film and the music, both are important. In India, a film and music are so intertwined and film has

effected so many, and vast, changes in Indian music that this requires a special study. Not only the development of films in India is very fascinating – in about 70 years, India stands perhaps as the largest producer of films, and music, the changing music, is an integral part of films. Films' contribution to music and culture is immense.

Even now, the film music is most dominating, most recorded, most sold and perhaps most exported music in the country. Not that all film music is light or the new music; a sizable part of it has been and still is classical or based on classical modes; but the spectrum extends from this to the latest 'fashion' songs. In between these two extremes, a wide variety of music is used in films and a considerable part thereof has so much contributed to the development of music in this country that it has become part of our musical archives. The film music has not only preserved the traditional music and made it more appealing by presenting it in new forms, but has also given rise to several new compositions, musical styles, musicians and music directors as well as composers who have blazed new trails with their creativity and experiments. For instance, the instrumental background music and the orchestral music are largely the contributions of cinema and are the result of its on-going search for new dimensions to utilise the richness of the Indian music in its various forms, blended occasionally with the new and modern. It is felt that a depth study in film and music in India will not only supplement the present study but will be a fascinating study itself of the development of music in India, especially the recorded music, its changes through time, its impact on the audience and *vice versa* - that is, the impact of the audience behaviour on the cinema music.

4. It seems that a study of intercultural penetration can be extremely informative. One study which may be suggested here is the use of North Indian music in South India and *vice versa* on various socio-economic variables. As stated somewhere in this report, the South Indian and the North Indian music, though derived from the same ancient sources, have lately developed more or less as two distinct streams. A study of this type will not only be useful for intercultural appreciation but will also throw light on the movement of culture from one

region to another, various factors which influence culture and the process of culture contact.

5. Evaluation of the existing cultural policies and analysis of their various aspects, considering them as a system in which the different components play a part. The communication model we have in mind presupposes three important elements – music-makers (artists/producers), music-receivers (consumers), and the technology users (the industry). The ancillary forces which impinge on this system are the cultural, organisational and environmental factors. It is expected that a comprehensive study of this type, even in parts, would be useful and indicative of how a cultural system develops in a particular ground, besides making an evaluation of the entire system showing its impact, usefulness, relevance and gaps, if any, which need attention.

NOTES

1. Eye Spy, *Multi-nationals again*, 1985.
2. Bade Ghulam Ali Khan, one of the greatest vocalists of recent times, was denied his demands for about 6 months and when he agreed to sing because of his failing health, cajolery and his interest in leaving his voice for posterity, his voice was not the same as it was 6 months earlier (Joshi, 1984; p. 61).

   Surashri Kesarbai Kerkar, another great artist, wanted to re-record a few songs as she felt that what was recorded was not to her standards. The recording was delayed for about 6 months. The boss of the company 'became very restive and wondered that Kesarbai, a mere artist, should have the audacity to disregard the wishes of a world-famous gramophone company (HMV)'. (*ibid.*, p. 151).

   This boss was described by another great artist, Begum Akhtar, as *Kudon ke badshah* (translated by the author as the 'king of fools' but more appropriately a derogatory remark, literally, 'the garbage-king'. (*ibid.* p. 152).

   Kesarbai Kerkar, when confronted with this attitude, severed all relationships with the company and she withdrew all rights to play her records on the All India Radio and the result was that there was not even one L.P. of this great artist with the HMV, the artist who was given the honorific, *Gantapaswini* – a lady singer totally dedicated to her art. (*ibid.* pp. 150-153).

   When Shanta Apte, one of the most talented singer-actresses of her time, ended her contract with the HMV and began to accept offers from elsewhere, HMV management was obviously upset. Desirous of weaning her away from others and bringing her back again in their fold, they played a trick which was as good as bribing her: they made a back-door entry through her brother and her signatures were taken when all were in an inebriated state. The writer, Joshi, who did not drink was the 'bar-man'. (*ibid.*, p.28).

   Some responses from our interviews: some artists felt 'cheated'; some felt 'big companies cared only for big artists'; and one states, 'he would never go to . . .'

3. A small entrepreneur told the writer that in a way, they were encouraging the new artists to come up. By offering novel and unconventional contract terms, and by suitable flexibility in bargaining, they got new source-material, and the performer or the new entrant got a welcome break which probably would result in getting him more public contracts and offers for live performances, and would also help them to jack up their prices the next time they would come. Here he was following — though perhaps he was not aware of this — a well-known marketing dictum: a good bargain is one where both the parties involved feel satisfied and happy.

   In this context of the importance of knowing the market needs and their reactions, a project by Nithyanadam (1981) on 'Market Survey of Dealers on New Product Introduction' may be mentioned where he carried the survey on the marketing practices and brand images of 7 phonogram producers (EMI, AVM, INDREMA, SEA, Sangeetha, Polydor, and Pirates). In spite of our best efforts we could not get the report of findings; however, we got the instrument — a questionnaire. It enquired (from dealers) about: (i) product position, (ii) pricing, (iii) dealer's margin, (iv) policies of the company, (v) liaison with sales representatives, (vi) promotional activities, (vii) consumer preferences, (viii) supplies, and (ix) a profile of each company on a 9-point scale, consisting of 7 dimensions — market share, reputation, stability of prices, quality, distribution and advertisement, quality as well as quantity.
4. See responses to Questionnaires 2 and 3, and Tables 17-A, and 18.
5. See note 11 of Chapter 1, for relevant text of the legislation. It is a welcome legislation but several interviewees had some reservations about its effectiveness in curbing piracy because of lengthy procedures, expensive and time-consuming court cases and possibility of non-detection and non-implementation even when its violation is detected.
6. Like books, whose import-export is freely allowed without many controls and whose production is encouraged; or, like cinematographic films, where license to import raw films is given.

   In this connection, we may mention the General Conference of UNESCO, Nairobi, 1976 — 99 years after the invention of phonograms — for a protocol to be adopted which, at last, recognises sound recordings as cultural material qualifying for all the privileges and protection so long enjoyed by books. (Comper, 1977).
7. The royalty rates, according to our information, vary from 10 per cent to 12.5 per cent on each cassette or record sold and is paid to producer in case of films; the music director is also paid a lump sum.

   On basic records, the royalty rates vary from 5 per cent (?) to 12.5 per cent depending on artists, their popularity, status and other considerations. The rates may vary from company to company and the royalty is split among the artist, lyric-writer and the music director. One of the largest consumer of phonograms is the All India Radio, which, we understand, pays Rs. 2.00 per song per broadcast. This is directly paid to the recording company (in case of film records, AIR pays royalty direct to producer). What the artist gets depends upon the former's contract with the company and it is not a direct concern of the AIR. Royalty on International music imports is paid to a collecting agency — Performing Rights Society—which has a branch in Bombay, who collects and distributes this royalty through its London office.

8. News, *Film Information*, of 24th Aug. 1985.
9. See Table 17-C (industry and artists), Table 18 (perception of the artists), and the following extract of a report by 'Eye Spy;' 85: 'I was shocked to hear that some of the multi-national music companies have not been paying the royalty due to the producers whose songs they market.'
10. An artist felt, they are being 'used'; some industry representatives were also quite emphatic that artists get a raw deal: An artist complained that he saw his record selling in the USA, about which he was never informed (!). 'We do not know how they keep the accounts.' There are a number of such responses which show dissatisfaction. This keeps artists away and alienated, and this feeling has to get expressed somewhere, in some way.
11. A fixed royalty of Rs. 2.00 per song per broadcast (revised in 1983) is given to the producer or the recording company. What the artist gets depends on his contract with company/producers. Remuneration for programmes recorded direct by AIR are governed by two types of contracts — CBF (Complete Broadcasting Fee), or SBF (Subsequent Broadcasting Fee) — in which each subsequent broadcast is paid for at some fraction of the initial fee. For Western Music Records, royalty rates are different, and they vary monthly, sometimes weekly. Royalty is paid to Performing Rights Society.

6

SUMMARY

AN INITIAL objective of this study was to assess the cultural role of phonograms in India. It was felt that such a study would be useful not only as an extension of several studies done in the West, but would also provide an insight into the contributions which the phonograms are making in diffusion of cultural communication, changing consumer behaviour and market strategies relevant thereto.

The study began with examining how it all began; and how the phonogram came to India. That it was readily accepted by the Indian people and became a useful technology, was not only due to the inherent quality of this technological invention but also because of the vast changes which India was experiencing at the turn of the century. She was willing to accept new cultural impacts of the West combined with her own spirit of coping with cultural changes which she had been continuously doing for several centuries in the past.

As the next step, it was tried to locate the industries engaged in the phonogram production – records and cassettes both. We discovered about 42 organisations, 16 of which were the members of the Indian Phonographic Industry (IPI) and the rest outside that federation. The major distinction between the two was that the majority of the organisations covered by the IPI were large-sized, included three multinationals which existed in the country, and contained most of the traditional and established companies, many of which started operating as early as the first decade of the present century. Gramophone Co. of India Ltd., more popularly known by its label "His Master's Voice" was the largest and the oldest and is still enjoying that status though its share in output and turnover, and its structure, all have undergone vast changes due to the emergence of new organisations and post-independence Indian laws.

Three instruments for data collection were prepared. Questionnaire 1 was the main instrument for collecting data from various industries about releases, production, sales, export and import – the releases were categorised according to the language and type of music. This questionnaire was sent to all the 42 organisations but the responses were received from only 22. For the sake of convenience and because of the almost clear distinction between the IPI and non-IPI organisations, the information was spilt in these two major categories. The information received is shown arranged in various ways in Tables 1 to 16 and discussed in chapter 4.

Questionnaires 2 and 3 were interview schedules for industry personnel and artists respectively. The former inquired about industrial personnel's perception about some of the issues concerning them:

(i) motivational urges and general outlook,
(ii) relationship with government,
(iii) relationship with artists,
(iv) copyright,
(v) export-import,
(vi) problems facing the industry, and
(vii) future of the industry.

They were also asked to give their suggestions.

The Questionnaire 3 for the artists employed 20 items in a 5-point scale of Strongly Agree – Strongly Disagree continuum and was concerned with several matters related to the artists – their relationship with industry, their cultural outlook on the role of phonograms, royalty and contracts etc. The number who responded was 9 for Questionnaire 2, and 11 for Questionnaire 3. The number was too small for any statistical inference but was certainly indicative of the thinking going on in the industry and among the artists about the problems closest to them. These data were supplemented by personal interviews with some significant people from industry and from among the artists, and experts. The analysis and findings based on these 2 questionnaires have been discussed in chapter 4.

Chapter 5 deals with our conclusions and general observations based upon the total picture deduced from the questionnaires, interviews and other sources. Briefly, some of the salient findings are as under:

(i) that film music still dominates, though the share of the monopoly houses is going down because of the emergence of various companies, during the past 15 years or so – both IPI (large-size including multi-nationals) and non-IPI (mostly medium-sized) organisations, which mainly run as individual enterprises.

(ii) there was an abrupt and steep decline during early eighties in the IPI members' output and turnover, due probably to the rampant proliferation of piracy which still dogs the industry in spite of several legal provisions and penalties, and also due to the appearance of tapes. However, cassettes are gradually gaining in film music while records seem more or less to maintain their position in other kinds of music categories.

(iii) new emerging companies seem to explore in new areas of music categories which were either neglected or only minimally tapped, especially the devotional and semi-classicals which are quite appealing to the people at large.

(iv) the erstwhile traditional compensation systems of royalty and contracts are now undergoing a change. While previously there was almost no competition, now there is; moreover, there is more awareness in artists about their rights and position.

(v) the biggest problem facing the industry is piracy. Many have suggested the ways to fight this evil not only through legislations and governmental interventions but also by their own efforts such as coordination and cooperation, and better relations with artists. Some have suggested competition and taxation reforms. Artists have also expressed that they have a role to play themselves in curbing this evil. It is heartening that an awareness is dawning that any social evil like this has to be fought by a concerted effort of all concerned.

In this connection the status of artists, their grievances, and their relationship with industry were also discussed. The artists seem to feel that they are more treated like 'items of trade' rather than living resources and an integral part of the whole system. This attitude of the industry is now undergoing a change due to competition and several new organisations coming up with new ideas and new attitudes which consider the cooperation of artists essential. Many of these new organisations are managed with professional expertise.

The last section mentions some significant areas emerging from this report, where further studies can be useful.

APPENDICES

APPENDIX A

A CONCISE HISTORY OF THE PHONOGRAPH INDUSTRY IN INDIA

G.N. JOSHI

THOUGH GRAMOPHONES were imported in India before the beginning of the century, this was done privately by very few persons who were very rich and affluent. During their visits to Europe and other Western countries they brought with them Gramophone machines for use at home because it was an attractive piece of novelty and a handy medium of entertainment. Therefore, in the year 1900 and thereafter also for quite some time a Gramophone machine was considered to be a show piece and a status symbol, because only the very rich and elite of the society could afford to possess it. Phonograph was commercially exploited in India only after the establishment of an office, by the Mutoscope Biograph Company in Calcutta, on July 7, 1901. This was done by one Mr. J. Watson Harrod.

Mr. Emili Berliner, an American, erected the first record pressing factory at Hanover in U.S.A. and he began to make a steady supply of records and machines to the Gramophone Co. Ltd. that was established in London around 1898. At this point a mechanic named Johnson invented a spring wound motor for a phonograph machine. Until this time, during the period when the record was being played, a listener was required to rotate the disc manually. But the new invention of spring wound motor enabled the phonograph to be played for a certain number of rotations and hence the listener could sit at a distance without having to bother to crank the machine by hand, all the time. In the initial stages recording for a gramophone was done by a process of "Zinc Etching". A zinc disc with a smooth and shiny surface was coated with a layer of fat on which spiral grooves were cut by a stylus. The stylus was fixed to a diaphragm that vibrated in sympathy with sound waves of the song and music, sung or played into the large mouth of a horn. The recorded zinc disc was then immersed in acid for about 10 minutes and the spiral grooves of music were etched on the surface. This disc record could then be played back straight away.

In 1901, recording on wax was invented and it became possible to duplicate the matrices so that large quantities could be copied from these. The process opened an enormous field for expansion. Around the year 1902, one Mr. F.W. Gaisberg came out to India for developing Gramophone record trade in this country. On arrival he made varied types of recordings by the then available Indian talent and these records are considered to be a landmark of immense value. Among the very first artists so recorded by him are still remembered the names of Misses Dulari, Gaurajan, Zohrajan, Malkajan, Angurbala, Indubala, Kamalazaria, Goharjan, Jankeebai, Mustaribai, etc. Amongst males were Pyaru Quawwal, Kalu Quawwal, Fakre Alam Quawwal, etc. The accompaniments for these artists comprised of just few instruments – a harmonium, a *tabla*, a *sarod*, a clarionet and, with female singers, a *sarangi* and bells. These recordings were then sent by Mr. Gaisberg for processing and pressing to the factory at Hanover in America. The finished records were then imported back into India and then on account of their fascinating novelty of reproducing a very faithful human voice, were sold in large numbers. In order to persuade likely purchasers to listen to the records to the end, another novel idea was tried out. At the end of the record and close of the singing, these artists were made to announce, his or her name, in 'English' as 'My name is Jankibai of Ilahabad' or 'My name is Mushtaribai of Agra'. These announcements in English by performers who did not know English language at all, amused the listeners and helped to boost the sales of records. The early machines were black in colour with a fantastic horn. A little later horns were made of brass and also in various bright colours. Gramophone machines with such impressive horns were known as 'Morning Glory' and became a rage around 1907.

In 1908, first factories were established at Belliaghat in Calcutta and also at Hayes, Middlesex in U.K. For the fast growing market, in India, amongst the first imported foreign discs, were Comic records known as 'Laughing song' recorded by Bert Shepard and this record as also others by Charles Primrose containing Route-march songs, Bugle calls, Campfire songs, Peanut Butter songs etc. gave huge sales and proved to be great money spinners. These were marketed under different labels such as "Pathé, R.C.C., Decca, Pye, etc.". Soon afterwards, it obtained exclusive rights to use in India, the trade-mark

"His Master's Voice". The dog and the phonograph is today the most famous trade-mark in the world. And the real story behind this picture is very interesting. An artist named Francis Barraud noticed one day that a dog belonging to his dead brother Mark Barraud would cock one ear to the sound emanating from an Edison phonograph. The expression of the dog suggested that it was waiting to hear his late master's voice. Francis Barraud painted the scene as he saw it. He named the picture "The Nipper and the Edison Machine". When shown to the Edison company they did not show much interest in it. So he repainted the black machine in the picture with a modern horn. In 1899, he called at the small office of the Gramophone Co. Ltd. and showed the picture to the manager B. Owen. The manager immediately grasped the potential it held as a trade mark for the company, paid £ 100 to Mr. Francis and obtained the picture for the company. Soon afterwards when records with the dog and sound horn appeared with the caption "His Master's Voice", the trade-mark won fame and popularity unparalleled in the history of the industry. It was printed on millions of records and machines in several countries in the world. In India it first appeared on a portable machine in 1920; later it was printed on the first electrical record produced by the company. Thus, the abbreviated letters "H.M.V." for "His Master's Voice" became synonymous with the organisation, the Gramophone Co. Ltd. The name "Gramophone Co. Ltd." was given to the factory at Belliaghat as well as the present Company at Hayes in England. The fast increase in sales of discs necessitated the shifting of the Belliaghat factory to a much bigger one and thus was established in 1928 a real large record-producing factory-complex at Dum Dum. It assured continuous progress as well as fast expansion for the future gramophone industry.

Technological Developments

The first electrical recording was introduced in India in the year 1925 when microphones, amplifiers and cutting stylus were used for recording the "Masters" on wax. A round disc of wax shaved to a mirror finish used to be placed on a turn-table which was driven at a fixed speed of 78 R.P.M. through a governor driven device. A heavy weight attached to a pully, descending slowly, through a cable wound around a drum, would rotate the turn-table at a steady speed of 78 R.P.M. This process of recording "Masters" has brought about a miraculous change in the technology of recording. The voice of the singers and accompanying instruments could be controlled and what is called a balance between the two could be achieved. In those days there were no studios with good acoustics and recording engineers were required to arrange heavy curtains on the walls and thick carpets on the floors, to ensure that the sound on the disc was neither too dull nor too reverberant. Later on studios were set up at Dum Dum, Calcutta; Bombay; Madras and Delhi. The recorded discs from the studios at these various centres were dispatched by railway wagons, to the factory in Dum Dum, for processing. This resulted on many occasions into breakages in transit. But despite this risk, wax recording held sway till about 1948. To minimise hazards of such breakages, acetate-coated aluminium discs were tried for some time. But the weight drive could not provide the requisite power to cut the coated material which was very much stiffer than wax. Thereafter, an electric motor was introduced for this purpose. Around 1950, came the revolutionary magnetic tape recorder, with a frequency response of 50 to 10,000 cycles per second. This recorder also provided facilities for playing back the recorded material. The merits and flaws of the recorded piece could then be noted and mistakes rectified through erasing the previously recorded attempts and re-recording afresh on the same tape. This resulted in improved sound quality in the performance without any loss except that of labour and time. By 1964 even better tape recorders with a frequency response between 40 to 15,000 cycles per second were introduced and, alongside, facilities were also provided for stereo-phonic recording.

The continent of India with a population of over 800 million and more than 30 languages and dialects has a vast treasure of musical tradition and colourful folklore. The company, therefore, had to scout and record as many artists as it could do. The rapidly growing popularity of the Gramophones and the discs demanded a very large supply of machines and records. This media of entertainment, which was considered once to be a luxury and a symbol of status, had now attracted the attention of even a common man. Until the year 1925 Gramophone machines used to be imported. Around 1928-29 cheap Japanese machines invaded the Indian market. A couple of years later dealers of the Gramophone Company, imported component parts of the machine from Switzerland and Japan. These then were used for assembling in locally made cheap wooden cabinets.

Monopoly and Threats of Competition

For over five decades the Gramophone Company enjoyed absolute monopoly of business. The Britishers, shrewd businessmen as they are, prevented a competition in the Gramophone trade by resorting to a very ingenious strategy. In Calcutta as well as other centres where they opened branches, they appointed some of the prominent and influential dealers to float small recording concerns having their individual names and labels. These dealers operated in the territories under their jurisdiction, selected artists who they thought were worthwhile from commercial angle, for selling their discs and arrange for their recordings in the studios of the Gramophone Co. Ltd. The processing of such recordings were done in the Dum Dum factory and the pressed records with individual labels of the different units were supplied to the dealers. In short, these units became sister companies of the main Gramophone Co. Ltd. In Calcutta Megaphone, Hindustan and Senola record companies were thus floated; in Madras, Hutchinson; in Bombay, Jai-Bharat and King record companies; in U.P., Maxitone, Aerophone and Star record companies; in Punjab, Jeinophone, Gulshan, Frontier Trading Company; in Rajasthan, Marwadi Record Company, etc. All these sister companies were floated at the instance of the Gramophone Company and were founded on the capital of their respective dealers so appointed. In fact all these different sister concerns were nourished and fostered by the Gramophone Co. Ltd. at no cost to them. This clever move of the Gramophone Company to corner and keep under its wings all available musical talent and business, throughout the length and breadth of this country, succeeded very well. These arrangements kept the factory all the time busy, bringing in fresh business from all corners of the nation. Thus, these helped the Gramophone Company to preserve its monopoly status for over fifty years thereafter. Apart from these, there were a few attempts outside the fold of the Gramophone Company to enter into the Gramophone world. A jeweller in Bombay around the year 1934 started his own concern under the label "broadcast". He gave fabulous amounts by way of fees to top highbrow artists and released the records in the market. These records being of classical nature did not have enough profitable pull in the market but discerning lovers of music welcomed their availability. However, the promoters of "broadcast" recording soon realised that the high fees paid to the artists did not make the continuance of the venture commercially viable and, therefore, they closed it down.

Around the year 1938 another competitive concern under the name National Record Company came into existence. The promoters of these were Indian business tycoons and they invited Japanese collaboration by obtaining machinery and technicians from Japan. The nationalised movement was year by year spreading. This record company enlisted the support of the Nation's leaders to back them in their venture. They succeeded in securing even the tri-colour national flag as their emblem and their trade mark as "Young India". Normally the Gramophone Company would not have bothered at the appearance of this competitive concern. But Mr. V. Shantaram, the Director of the Prabhat Film Company, Pune, who was an associate of the Gramophone Company was weaned away and defected to this National concern as a director. Mr. V. Shantaram in 1934 produced his first colour picture "Sairandhree". It contained several hit song numbers. Enterprising as he has always been, Mr. Shantaram went to Germany to obtain therefrom colour prints of his picture and while returning he also brought with him pressings of the songs in the form of Gramophone discs from this picture. These imported records from Germany, when released in Indian market, created a great sensation. It can be safely said that the appearance of these film records opened a vast future market for film music in this country. When V. Shantaram joined "Young India" – National Record Company, it gave a big jolt to the Gramophone Company. However, luckily for the Gramophone Company the Japanese technicians and machinery failed miserably to deliver the goods of standard and high quality, comparable to the high standard set up by the Gramophone Company. The poor quality of the finished records in material and the very disappointing quality of recording were very soon realised by customers at large, and, although for 3-4 years this record company made good business, then, ultimately they, too, had to down their shutters. Mr. V. Shantaram, rejoined H.M.V. Group and the prestige of the Gramophone Company rose very high.

Around the year 1932 Columbia and Odeon tried to enter and establish their labels in India. Columbia was a British venture and Odeon was of German origin. They had their own recording studios and their own engineers where they recorded Indian artists. The processing and pressing of these records were done in the U.K. and Germany respectively. Soon after, Columbia took over Odeon but later got amalgamated with Ruby Record Company which was established in 1938. Later in 1943 H.M.V. managed to take over the Ruby Record Company and along with it secured also the entire Columbia and Odeon repertoire. Columbia after that again raised its head and, being of British origin, formed an alliance with the Gramophone Company. Although it functioned administratively as an independent, the ultimate controlling directorate for both the companies were the same; therefore, the recordings and pressings were all looked after in the studios and factories of the Gramophone Company that fed both H.M.V. and Columbia labels and maintained its monopoly status.

In monthly joint meetings of the Gramophone Company and Columbia, the recording staff of both the concerns decided on fresh issues for ensuing months from the reserves and recordings made during the preceding period. While doing so, care was taken to finalise the issue of fresh records in such a manner that both H.M.V. and Columbia labels would be evenly balanced – 'sales wise'. On the standard H.M.V. and Columbia labels were issued recordings which would attract clientele from upper and middle classes of the social strata. For the consumption of lower middle and lower classes, the company issued records suitable to their tastes and requirements on cheaper labels known as TWIN for H.M.V. and REGAL for Columbia. At times old good sellers on the higher priced labels were, after years of fair sale, transferred on to these cheaper labels to retain them in catalogues and obtain additional sales in the market.

The Gramophone Company is now a Public Limited Company with 40 per cent of its shares held abroad. Sometimes back it was investigated by the Monopolies and Restrictive Trade Practices Commission and this, for the first time, put curbs on the monopolistic activities of the Gramophone Company. With the appearance of another foreign concern which had its origin in Germany and which secured also the help and collaboration of Dutch Philips Phonographic Industry under the name 'Polydor', came a real and genuine competitive threat to the Gramophone Company. This was in the late 1960s. Polydor succeeded in securing active and vested co-operation from a group of businessmen in Bombay known as "Patel Group". The 'Patel group' was well established in the trading of Cinema machinery and Photographic goods. It also conducted a cine-film processing laboratory. On account of this, this group was in close contact with the film producing industry. Between the years 1940 to 1960 their was a tremendous increase in the record business from Indian films. The Patels on account of their close contacts with the film industry managed to make recording agreements for 'Polydor' from quite a few film producers. The Patels, in addition, advanced lump sums to the film producers against royalties for the Gramophone discs. All this resulted in starting a regular warfare between the Gramophone Company and Polydor for exclusive recording rights. This writer remembers how we were set out to obtain long term contractual commitments from prominent and outstanding cinema producers and singer artists like Shanta Apte, Mohammed Rafi, Mukesh, Manna De, Lata Mangeshkar, Asha Bhosale, Suman Kalyanpur and several others. Polydor on account of Mr Patel's cooperation managed to make a big headway in the film records business. Even so, Gramophone Company on account of its very long existence in the field still held a dominant position. Gradually, however, with restrictions and curbs on recording and the exclusivity of contractual obligations of the artists, Gramophone Company suffered a great deal in both prestige and business. At present I understand that the prominent play back artists are covered only by temporary contracts and the exclusivity clause has now almost been removed.

Expansion of Record Trade and Business Tactics

After the first novelty of a Gramophone disc was worn out, the Gramophone Company for over half a century poured into the market records of various sorts, catering to various tastes of the heterogeneous population of this vast country. They tried to satisfy practically all the different and varied requirements of music lovers. Whatever artistic talent came their way was grabbed by the Gramophone Company and the recordings flooded the market. On account of their monopoly status, artists by and large felt happy and honoured on being recorded and did not press for commensurate remuneration in lieu of their performance. This writer too, when first recorded in the year 1932, was lured to the studios to record only two of his most popular songs. Actually, at the recording session, he became so involved and excited, at the prospect of being recorded that instead of just two songs when the recording session was wound up after about 6 hours, he discovered that he had recorded actually, instead of two, 14 songs! These songs when released in the market received such unprecedented support that literally thousands of discs were sold away, like hot cakes. Artists are by nature very simple, sentimental and temperamental. When this writer received such a tremendous following and public favour he did not care that he was not paid a single penny for the first 14 songs!

Performing artists in India were then mostly illiterate and ignorant of business tactics. They were carried away by the popularity of their recordings and the easy fame and name they got from the discs. After the first recording in 1932, this writer continued to record, at intervals, 10 to 12 titles each time, until the year 1938, on cash payment of a few hundred rupees. In 1935, as a token of appreciation for the phenomenal sales of his records, a gold-plated medal was awarded to him for being a best seller. The total cash received by him during all these years of his career as a Recording artist was around Rs. 3,000 only, although he had over seventy discs listed in his name and to his credit. It was only after this writer joined the Gramophone Company as a Recording Officer that for the first time, he became aware that the company had, besides the cash payment of paltry sums, another mode of remuneration in terms of royalty. *The practice of payment on royalty basis was a well guarded secret and this was offered only to big film clients.* "Every thing is fair in love, war and business"; acting on this well-known dictum, the company managed to get recordings from artists on very nominal cash payments and thus carried huge profits for their principals in England.

Gramophone as a Trend-setter and Changes in Consumer Interest

The Gramophone has served from time to time as a trend-setter. It is the psychology of masses all over the world to follow blindly the popular craze. Some years ago it was noticed in the Western countries that music lovers were affected by a Beatlemania, Rock-'n-roll, Disco, etc. In India too we had such waves of popularity in music. Towards 1920, in Maharashtra there was a craze for stage music. The stage music of Maharashtra was based on Hindustani Classical Music and great actors, singers like Balgandharva, Keshav Bhonsale, Master Dinanath, Pendharkar, etc. won tremendous following for their presentations in the musical dramas. The Gramophone company made huge earnings from these records of stage songs. Around 1932, when this writer appeared in the record market for the first time, he started a new trend in lyric singing. This vogue had such a tremendous impact on the both urban and rural listeners that '*Bhavageet*' singing ruled the hearts of listeners in Maharashtra for a number of years and he has been held a pioneer of lyric singing.

The stage music, as mentioned earlier, was based on classical music. Hence, the classical performances of artists having big names were also sought for. Most of the classical artists were uneducated and they held very conservative views and ideas. They did not, therefore, like the idea of putting their art on gramophone discs because they felt that their treasure of artistic knowledge would be cheapened by such recording. It was not very easy therefore, to persuade such artists to come to the recording studios. However, quite a few of them were recorded in those days when only 78 rpm discs were produced. These artists found it very difficult to present their great artistry in the short span of three and a half minutes (which was the limit of one side of a 78 rpm disc). Often they complained about this. Around the year 1968, long-play Microgroove recordings were introduced in Indian market. These were manufactured with plastic material and they were very light in weight and unbreakable. The performance time for a single side of a L.P. in those days was upto about 18 minutes which was nearly 5 times that of a single side of a 78 rpm record. It became easy, therefore, to induce the big shots, in the classical field, to come forward for recording. In the intervening period of nearly three decades, the general outlook also had considerably changed. I may be permitted to mention here that I was in the employment of the Gramophone Company from 1st June, 1938 for over 30 years and hence by the year the long play discs appeared on the scene, I was a most senior Recording Officer. Being a student and lover of classical Hindustani Music from childhood. I was very keen on recording as much of classical music and as many classical musicians as I could. Therefore, I decided to go all out to get all the top artists who had already made a grade.

However, the pure commercial aspect of the authorities in the Company many a times came in the way. Whenever I would make a proposal to record some distinguished vocalist or instrumentalist, the first question the bosses would ask me was, "how many records do you think, Mr. Joshi, would be sold in 3 months?" My arguments were in the following manner: In the first place, classical music is meant for classes and not for masses. It is not a cup of tea for a common and ordinary man; therefore, clientele for classical music was bound to be far less than the most popular music of the films. I had, therefore, to argue and make out strong case for recording the particular artists and on occasions I had to verbally fight with the bosses for obtaining the sanction. My argument would be that the records may not sell even 30 copies but the records of the films have a very short-lived life. These classical recordings would continue to be on the selling list, may be for more than 50 - 60 years – and this would give far much bigger over-all sales than the other records. And besides, where would the company get again an artist of such calibre and stature? Also, I pleaded that the company was exploiting the Indian talent purely from commercial angle since inception, as there was no competitor and if I was not allowed to do these recordings who would do this. The bosses usually made wry faces and told me not to bother about it. They would say, "Leave it to Government Agencies, All India Radio and other cultural organisations". However, after such heated arguments on most occasions I could have my way and I went ahead full steam getting almost all the available classical top notchers before the mike. Between the years 1968 and 1973, I succeeded in bringing before the mike almost every worthwhile classical musician.

What the Gramophone Company failed to do?

So far I have said what the Gramophone Company did during the last period of over six decades. I would now like to mention a few things which I feel Gramophone Company should have undertaken to do. Perhaps, if there was a keen competition from other concerns, this company might have looked beyond purely commercial aspect. Lack of any competition, ability to sell anything and everything that was put in the market, regardless of even some flaws, made the authorities complacent, satisfied, and without any enthusiasm to do something extraordinary. It may be pointed out here, that for the same reason the recording staff was made to work under conditions which needed vast improvements and better equipment.

Even the studios where recordings were done almost round the clock, were not accoustically up to the mark. The studio of the Gramophone Company, Bombay, located in the heart of the business sector, was not even completely soundproof. On several occasions recording sessions were required to be suspended because of extraneous noises filtering through. Even the dragging of chairs, on the floor directly above, would cause an irritati g noise resulting in the stoppage of recording. It became, therefore, necessary to arrange very important recordings at such hours in the morning or night or on holidays when we were sure that such interference would not be creeping.

As it was with the studios so also, more or less, it was with the equipment. Between the years 1950 and 1970 we did receive, periodically, machinery with advanced recording technology. The local staff used to be under the impression that these were absolutely the latest and the last word in recording. Actually it was later learned that as newly invented machinery was introduced in the most up to date and sophisticated offices in the parent country, the old machines that made room for the newly developed machinery and which were discarded from those studios were transshipped to the offices in India and not knowing that these were the old discarded ones we always felt elated. 'Polydor' made a headway in the market because they came out with products from the latest innovations in the recording technique, attractive packaging, artistic, original and skilful advertising. This progress and march onwards by the competitive company probably opened the eyes of the Gramophone Company and whatever improvements that are noticeable now are the results of the last 20 years or so.

The Gramophone Company did not, during the last over 80 years, pay any attention to build up a comprehensive library of discs and tapes. The authorities never looked beyond just a few years and, therefore, a colossal number of recordings of great historical and cultural importance are not now even traced. One would have thought that a vast organisation like the Gramophone Company doing roaring business would have the vision of looking far ahead for preservation and propagation of the culture of this country. Indian civilisation is regarded in the world today as one of the oldest with extremely rich heritage. It is a very sorry state of affairs that the company failed to preserve all that was the best in the cultural past for posterity and future.

The teeming millions of Indian rural population are still illiterate, without the facilities even to read or write and to have adequate means of subsistence. Although we have won the freedom more than 35 years ago, we have still to achieve a lot to eradicate illiteracy, poverty and develop the nation industrially and economically. India has probably now shown some remarkable progress amongst the nations which are considered to belong to the third and undeveloped world. A lot more remains to be achieved and now there are favourable signs with political stability and industrial advance, that India will rise very soon above the poverty line. For the broad mass of the Indian people, who are economically so poor and uneducated, a Gramophone machine is still an item of luxury. Its educational and cultural potential have yet to be fully realised and recognised.

Realising the role of a Gramophone machine in the education of younger generation this writer, way back during 1946-48, planned production of records of interest to children. A beginning was made with the release of 9 inch discs, low-priced to enable parents to purchase easily for their children and on subjects which would be of great interest and entertainment to kids. The label of these records had such captions as BAL (child); BODH (instruction) and RANJAN (entertainment). Bedtime stories, lullaby songs in mother tongues, and nursery rhymes were amongst the first issues. With a view to put before the youngsters ideals and achievements of giants in the literary, political, artistic and other fields, the scheme was chalked out for the issues of recordings containing "Lives and life works" of such distinguished persons. However, the masses and the society as also education authorities were not alive to the introduction of such records and, therefore, this experiment of the writer also failed. Similar fate awaited other experiments. Mention is made here only to bring to the notice of the authorities dealing with education the need to even now consider making such recordings.

Indian classical music was never taught in schools or colleges or through books. During the past few centuries, it has lived and thrived on the basis of *Guru Shishya Parampara* (Master-Pupil-Tradition); the great vocal and instrumental maestros that this country has produced were all tutored orally and personally by their masters. This was a process of continuous and ardous training lasting for a number of years. The British, when they took over India, did not care to offer adequate patronage to the great music masters and, therefore, this oral teaching tradition was neglected for years. With the spread of general education, more and more youngsters were attracted towards the art of classical music but due to the lack of adequate facilities for proper and able coaching, they were frustrated. This writer listened to the recordings made by "Lingua Franca" which were made for the teaching of different languages the easy way. It was, therefore, thought that if music lesson records on the same line are prepared, accompanied by informatory booklets, they would be welcome to customers. This writer, therefore, enlisted the cooperation of learned musicians known for their profound scholarship and with their help prepared a scheme and actually launched it. The first two records were made and issued under the caption *Sangeet Shiksha* (Musical training) on Columbia label. This scheme also failed for want of proper push, publicity, and support from both society and government and I was advised to desist from making such non-productive experiments and leave them to be tackled by socially conscious organisations and at more propitious times. It may be mentioned here that in the year 1964 this writer paid a visit to London, at his own cost, and during his stay there, was pleasantly surprised to find that the Head Office of the Gramophone Company in London was maintaining a separate educational records department for children. The vast repertoire of children's records, that was exhibited there, was an eye-opener, and this writer honestly felt that the Gramophone Company ought to have, out of sheer gratefulness and duty to the people of this country, done something for the coming generations. As it was with the cultural past, so it has been also with the coming generations. Isn't this very sad?

Introduction of Pre-recorded Cassettes and Their Impact

With the appearance of electronic gadgets like transistors, hi-fi stereophonic equipment, tape decks and cassette players, and with the all-round improvement in the standard of living in the developing countries, more and more Indians are now tempted to use these easily available gadgets of entertainment. The impact of alien music from the West or the East has been so great that consumers have discarded their old likes and are easily taking up to the new innovations in music composition and presentation. Hi-fi sophisticated equipments, although still very costly compared to the conditions prevailing a few years ago, have found favour with large number of now economically better placed people. Pre-recorded cassettes have now invaded the market with an astonishing speed and have almost replaced the Gramophone record trade in the Indian market. The easy availability, at fairly reasonable prices, of cassettes and cassette-players and their very simple and easy operation have been the main causes of their terrific impact. A cassette can easily be carried in pocket and a player also is so handy to carry, that one is tempted to use these in preference to the intricate and heavy-bulky Gramophone machine and the microgroove L.P. records. This innovation of cheap recording medium has found tremendous favour and it is likely that this will spread over very quickly. Masses in general preferred to enjoy music of reasonably good quality recorded and reproduced through the cassettes. They neither understand nor care much for the finer qualities in recording and reproduction. Therefore, a Gramophone machine and the record, both of which cost very much more than the cassette and the player, have a dim chance of survival.

Although it appears that the use of Gramophone and discs are on the wane in the Indian market, I still feel optimistic that this is only a temporary phase. The demand for Indian discs in the international market has increased manifold. Indian-made Gramophone records are marketed and are available in every corner of the world. Cassettes of the same recordings are also available in those countries but since the purchasing power of listeners in those countries is very much better, they prefer to go in for the Gramophone records along with also the cassettes which are so very cheap. Orders from outside India for Indian records are so large that the Gramophone companies at present doing business in India could register a phenomenal rise in their export trade in coming years. For the Indian people, as mentioned earlier, although a Gramophone and records are still items of luxury, it is hoped and expected that their educational and cultural potential could be fully realised and utilised, with the economic improvements and prosperity in coming years. The Phonograph brings to its owner a music of his choice and the music is always at his command.

It is, therefore, undoubtedly undisputable that the invention of Thomas Edison and Charles Cros has brought indescribable happiness to millions in this country.

APPENDIX B-1

INSTRUCTION BOOKLET

Introduction

THIS UNESCO sponsored study is undertaken by Behavioural Sciences Centre in collaboration with MEDIACULT – International Institute of Audio-visual Education and Cultural Development, Vienna.

This booklet explains the aim and use of the study, the scope and nature of the survey, the confidentiality in publication, the concepts and definitions used in this questionnaire, and gives instruction for answering individual questions.

Return your completed questionnaire within twenty days of receipt in the envelope provided. In case you encounter any difficulty, or need any assistance please contact:

Behavioural Sciences Centre, (011) 271584 and 263786.

Aim of the Study

The aim of this study titled "Phonogram in Cultural Communication in India", which is in line with similar studies done in other countries,[1] is to assess the role of phonogram in preserving and propagating the culture of our country. We want to know what role the industry has played in communicating the culture within our country as well as abroad.

The study is envisaged in two parts:

Part I

An objective fact finding survey of the industry to assess what has

1. Kurt Blaukopf, (ed.) *The Phonogram in Cultural Communication*, Springer-Verlag, Wien, (1982).
   Kurt Blaukopf, *Massenmedium Schallplatte*, Breitkopf & Härtel, Wiesbaden (1977).

been done during the last ten years.

Part II

An analysis of the views of the industry personnel, producers, artists, experts, governmental agencies and cultural policy makers on:

(a) the goal of the industry
(b) the role of the industry in cultural communication
(c) industry's relationship with producers, artists etc.
(d) the prevailing environment in the industry
(e) the future of the industry

Special Importance is attached to an Assessment of the Problems and Challenges the Industry is facing Today

This questionnaire serves the first part of the study.

Use of this Study

The result of this study is expected to be helpful to the industry as well as the government in creating awareness and in formulating policies which may help further developing the phonogram as a significant and powerful medium of cultural communication.

Scope and Nature of the Survey

This is a survey of the following activities engaged in by the recording industry: Production, release and sale of records and pre-recorded cassettes; import and export of master tapes, records and pre-recorded cassettes. The object of this survey is to determine the quantity and content of records and cassettes released as well as those imported and exported, during the last ten years.

Confidentiality in Publication

Results of this survey will be released in such a form that would not allow either the direct or indirect disclosure of any individual company's contribution to the volume or value of any production. The Centre will ensure that the information received from individual organisation remains strictly confidential, and will be released only to the extent permitted by the reporting organisation.

Concepts and Definitions used in the Survey Reporting Organisation

This is the corporate entity identified by your company name. Under no circumstances should an Indian subsidiary of a foreign record company consider the parent company to be the reporting organisation.

A Master

An original sound recording or any generation of an original sound recording used in the manufacture of records or pre-recorded cassettes. Usually this is a master tape.

To Release a Record

To arrange for the pressing of discs or the duplication of tapes in either your company owned facilities or by a custom pressing arrangement with a pressing plant.

Indian Music

A musical selection is deemed to be Indian if it qualifies under any two of the following conditions:

(A) The instrumentation or lyrics were principally performed by an Indian.
(B) The music was composed by an Indian.
(C) The lyrics were written by an Indian, and
(D) The live performance was wholly recorded in India.

International Music

Any music that is not 'Indian' (see above 'Indian music') is considered international music in this survey.

Cassettes

Here mean pre-recorded cassettes.

Guide to Questionnaire

Question 2: The total number of employees refers to all those who work for your head office and any branch offices in the country including officers.

Question 4: "Controlling interest" is the ability or potential ability of an individual, a group of individuals or a company to determine the operating and financial policies of the reporting organisation including the ability to select the majority of the reporting organisation's directors.

Question 6,7,8, Re-issues of older material should be counted as a new release only if it has a separate catalogue number from the original.

Question 6: (a) Category of Music
Indian Music (excluding Indian Classical music)

- (i) Film music: Film story sets, film tunes, popular tunes, orchestra etc.
- (ii) Semi-Classical Music: Geet, ghazals, dadras, thumri, quawwali, light songs.
- (iii) Folk songs
- (iv) Devotional songs
- (v) Children's songs, Educational programmes
- (vi) Miscellaneous: dramas, operas, stage songs, patriotic songs, Tagore compositions, speeches etc.

(b) Other formats in disc
Include 45 RPM L.P., 45 RPM E.P., S.P. Super 7 etc.

Use one sheet for one language. Ask for more sheets if needed.

Question 7: Indian classical music:
Hindustani (North Indian), Carnatic (South Indian), vocal, Instrumental.

Question 8: (i) Pop music: Rock music, disco music, dance music etc.

(ii) Country music:

(iii) Serious music: Western classical music, Jazz music etc.

(iv) Any other

Respondents are asked to use their own judgement when classifying music.

Question 9: Manufactured by your company owned facilities or by a custom pressing arrangement with another plant.

APPENDIX B-2

PHONOGRAM AND CULTURAL COMMUNICATION IN INDIA

QUESTIONNAIRE 1

SURVEY OF THE RECORDING INDUSTRY: 1975-1984

PLEASE REFER to the Instruction Booklet before completing the questionnaire. Please answer all questions. If the answer to a particular question is zero, indicate by a "0" in the appropriate box; if not available or unknown enter a "U".

Please return this questionnaire within twenty days of receipt of this request.

This questionnaire is to be completed by the head office of your organisation.

Eligibility to Report

Your organisation is eligible to report if it undertakes any one of the following activities: (Please tick mark the activities you undertake)

1. Release of records (see definition in instruction booklet)
2. Release of cassettes
3. Sale of records
4. Sale of cassettes
5. Importing of master tapes
6. Importing of records/cassettes

Preliminary Description of Reporting Organisation

1. Indicate how long this organisation has been established in

India.

(a) Less than two years
(b) Two to five years
(c) Six to ten years
(d) Over ten years

2. Indicate the number of branch offices and the number of employee of this organisation.

   Branches:
   Employee:

3. Is this organisation a subsidiary of another organisation? If 'Yes', give the name of the parent company and its location.
4. Indicate, if any, the country in which the controlling interest of this organisation is located.
5. Indicate the category of the legal status of this organisation (check only one)

   (a) Sole proprietorship
   (b) Partnership
   (c) Co-operative
   (d) Incorporated organization not for profit
   (e) Incorporated organization for profit-Public
   (f) Incorporated organization for profit-private
   (g) other (specify) ——————

RELEASES

TABLE I: **Indian Music (excluding Indian Classical Music)**
6. Indicate the number of releases (not quantity of records) according to language, category of music and format. (See definition in instruction booklet)

Language . . .

Category (i) Film Music					*Category (ii) Semi-classical music*				
Year	33 1/3 RPM L.P.	Other formats in disc	Casse-tte	Total (1+2+3)	Year	33 1/3 RPM L.P.	Other formats in disc	Casse-tte	Total (1+2+3)
	1	2	3	4		1	2	3	4
1975					1975				
1976					1976				
1977					1977				
1978					1978				
1979					1979				
1980					1980				
1981					1981				
1982					1982				
1983					1983				
1984					1984				
Total					Total				

(1) Category of music, format: Please see instruction booklet.
(2) If a programme is released in both a disc and tape format, count it only once and enter it in the column for L.P.
Use one sheet for one language.

Category (iii) Folk Songs					*Category (iv) Devotional Songs*				
Year	33 1/3 RPM L.P.	Other formats in disc	Casse-tte	Total (1+2+3)	Year	33 1/3 RPM L.P.	Other formats in disc	Casse-tte	Total (1+2+3)
	1	2	3	4		1	2	3	4
1975					1975				
1976					1976				
1977					1977				
1978					1978				
1979					1979				
1980					1980				
1981					1981				
1982					1982				
1983					1983				
1984					1984				
Total					Total				

(Contd.)

TABLE I *(Contd.)*

Category (v) Children's songs, Educational programmes					*Category (vi) Miscellaneous*				
Year	33 1/3 RPM L.P.	Other formats in disc	Casse-tte	Total (1+2+3)	Year	33 1/3 RPM L.P.	Other formats in disc	Casse-tte	Total (1+2+3)
	1	2	3	4		1	2	3	4
1975					1975				
1976					1976				
1977					1977				
1978					1978				
1979					1979				
1980					1980				
1981					1981				
1982					1982				
1983					1983				
1984					1984				
Total					Total				

TABLE II: **Indian Classical Music**
7. Indicate the number of releases in Indian Classical Music according to category and format.

	Hindustani					*Carnatic*					
Year	Vocal		Instru-mental		Total (1+2)	Vocal		Instru-mental		Total (4+5)	Total (3+6)
	R	C	R	C		R	C	R	C		
	1		2		3	4		5		6	7
1975											
1976											
1977											
1978											
1979											
1980											
1981											
1982											
1983											
1984											
Total											

R = Records C = Cassettes

Note: If a programme is released in both a disc and tape format, count it only once, and enter it under the column for Record.

TABLE III: **International Music**

8. Indicate the number of releases (not quantity of records) in International music according to category and format.

Year	Popular music		Country music		Serious music		Other		Total
	R	C	R	C	R	C	R	C	
1975									
1976									
1977									
1978									
1979									
1980									
1981									
1982									
1983									
1984									
Total									

R = Records C = Cassettes

Note: If a programme is released in both a disc and tape format, count it only once, and enter it under the column for 'R'.

TABLE IV: **Production**

9. Indicate the number of records and cassettes produced according to category of music. (Figure in thousands).

Year	Film music	Class-ical music	Semi-Class-ical music	Folk songs	Devoti onal songs	Child-ren's Educat-ional	Miscel-laneous	Interna-tional music	Total
1975									
1976									
1977									
1978									
1979									
1980									
1981									
1982									
1983									
1984									
Total									

R = Records C = Cassettes

TABLE V: **Sale**

10. Indicate the number of records and cassettes sold. (Specify the figure, in thousands)

Year	Records	Cassettes	Total
1975			
1976			
1977			
1978			
1979			
1980			
1981			
1982			
1983			
1984			
Total			

TABLE VI: **Import**

11. Indicate the number of master tapes imported and the country of import.

Country	1975	1976	1977	1978	1979	1980	1981	1982	1983	1984	Total

TABLE VII: **Export**: Indian Music (inlcuding all categories)
12. Indicate the number of records and cassettes exported according to the content of music and the country of export. (Specify the figure, in thousands)

Country	1975		1976		1977		1978		1979		1980		1981		1982		1983		1984		To-tal
	R	C	R	C	R	C	R	C	R	C	R	C	R	C	R	C	R	C	R	C	

R = Records. C = Cassettes.

TABLE VIII: **Export**: International Music (inlcuding all categories)
13. Indicate the number of records and cassettes exported and the country of export. (Specify the figure, in thousands)

Country	1975		1976		1977		1978		1979		1980		1981		1982		1983		1984		To-tal
	R	C	R	C	R	C	R	C	R	C	R	C	R	C	R	C	R	C	R	C	

R = Records. C = Cassettes.

Your Suggestions and Comments:

Please note down your suggestions and comments which you think will supplement the data.

APPENDIX C

PHONOGRAM AND CULTURAL COMMUNICATION IN INDIA

QUESTIONNAIRE 2

RECORDING INDUSTRY

Dear . . .

BEHAVIOURAL SCIENCES Centre is engaged in a research study on the role of 'Phonogram in Cultural Communication in India.' This is sponsored by UNESCO, and is done in collaboration with MEDIACULT – International Institute for Audio Visual Communication and Cultural Development, Vienna. This questionnaire which is an integral part of the study is meant to elicit free and uninhibited views on the industry in general, its goal, its role in cultural communication, its relationship with the government, with the artists, producers etc., import and export of phonograms, the problems the industry is facing today, and the future challenges.

As a person experienced in this field your answers to the questionnaire will be considered a valuable contribution to the study. You can note down your answers on the questionnaire itself or on a separate sheet of paper. *Please make use of the space for suggestions and comments on the last page where you can record your observations, experiences, and concerns which you think will enrich the study.* Answers will be confidential. You will not be quoted in the report without your prior permission. Please send the completed questionnaire as early as possible to:

BEHAVIOURAL SCIENCES CENTRE
32, NETAJI SUBHASH MARG
NEW DELHI-110002.

We shall be grateful to you for your kind co-operation.

Confidential

Name ——————————
Address ——————————
Designation ——————————

1. How many years have you been in the Industry?
2. How do you feel being in the Industry?
3. Do you think the industry is growing or is it retarding?
4. What are the negative trends in the Industry?
5. What are the positive trends in the Industry?
6. What do you think is the goal of the Phonographic Industry?
   (a) Primary goal
   (b) Secondary goal
7. What do you think about the role of Phonogram in cultural communication?
8. What role does the Industry play in the development of culture in India?
9. Does your company have a cultural policy of its own? If yes, explain the policy.

RECORDING INDUSTRY AND THE GOVERNMENT

10. Are you satisfied with the cultural policy of the Government with regard to the Industry? If not, what changes would you like to have?
11. Do you think there is a general lack of awareness about the recording industry among Government Departments?
12. Do you think the Government considers the phonogram as important a medium as film, books etc. for cultural communication?

RELATIONSHIP WITH ARTISTS, PRODUCERS ETC.

13. Do you think the artists/Producers are satisfied with the Industry?

What are the reasons for satisfaction or dissatisfaction?

(a) Royalty terms
(b) Prestige of the Company
(c) Credibility of the Company
(d) Personal relationship with the Company Officials
(e) any other

14. Do you think there is scope for improving the relationship? How?
15. Do you think the industry should have uniform policy on royalty?
16. Do you think royalty rates should be same for all artists irrespective of their popularity and social prestige?
17. Do you think the policy of exclusive contracts needs to be reviewed? If yes, give reasons.
18. Do you have any suggestion on the system of contracts?

COPYRIGHT

19. What do you think about the copyright amendment act of October 1984? Is it an effective one?
20. Do you think it has been effectively implemented?
21. What are the problems in the implementation of this act?
22. What is the role to be played by the Government in this regard?
23. What is the role to be played by the industry in this regard?

IMPORT-EXPORT

(Answer questions 25-29 only if your organisation imports master tapes or exports records/cassettes)

24. How does the Government policy affect import and export of phonograms?
25. What changes would you wish in the import-export policy of the Indian Government?
26. What type of music do you import: more of serious music or pop music? Why?
27. What type of music you export: more of Indian music or International music? Why?

28. What are the guiding factors for other countries for importing phonograms for India? Specify:
    (a) Economic reasons.
    (b) Political reasons.
    (c) Cultural reasons.

29. Do you think there is a growing interest in Indian music among foreigners? Substantiate your answer with data if possible.

PROBLEMS FACING THE INDUSTRY

30. What are the most important problems facing the industry today?
31. What are your suggestions to tackle each of these problems?
32. Do you think the public is aware of these problems? If not, what you think is to be done.

FUTURE OF RECORDING INDUSTRY

33. What do you think is the future of the recording industry?
34. What do you think are the future Challenges to the Industry?
35. Please Note Down Your Comments And Suggestions.

APPENDIX D

PHONOGRAM AND CULTURAL COMMUNICATION IN INDIA

QUESTIONNAIRE 3

RECORDING ARTISTS

Name ______________________

Address ______________________

____

____

Age ______________________

Sex ______________________

Occupation ______________________

1. Please tick mark the activity you do in recording:
   (a) Singing
   (b) Playing musical instrument (Please specify the instrument)
   (c) Singing and Playing musical instrument
2. How many years have you been singing/playing for professional recording?
3. In the past have you performed under exclusive contract with any company? If 'Yes', specify:
   (a) Company's name:
   (b) Duration of contract:
4. At present are you under contract with any company? If 'Yes' specify:
   (a) Company's name:
   (b) Duration of contract:
5. Are you satisfied with your relationship with the recording companies? (tick mark only one)
   Yes: (give reasons)
   No: (give reasons)

Given below are a set of statements. Mark your agreement or disagreement with the statement in the following way:
Strongly Agree (SA), Agree (A), Undecided (U),
Disagree (D), Strongly Disagree (SD).

You may write your answer by using the short forms.

1. The importance of phonogram as a medium of cultural communication is very well recognised by the industry as well as the public.
2. The primary intention of the recording companies as far as I know is the promotion of artists and styles of music.
3. Recording companies should make maximum use of the talents of the popular and established artists rather than going for new and younger artists.
4. Promoting younger and new artists involves great financial risk and hence should be done discreetly.
5. The system of exclusive contract with a particular company for a definite period of time should be discontinued.
6. Artists should be free to sing for any company they like.
7. Artists can be paid royalty on every record/cassette sold even without entering into exclusive contract with the company.
8. The recording companies keep very good relationship with their artists.
9. Recording companies take special care of those artists who are under exclusive contract with their companies.
10. Recording companies are concerned about the personal well-being of the artists.
11. Remuneration given by the recording companies is reasonable.
12. The company officials are faithful in matters of payment of royalty.
13. Royalty rates should be the same for all artists irrespective of their popularity and prestige.
14. There should be uniform royalty rates for all companies.
15. Flat payment for each programme at the time of recording is better than royalty payments.
16. Recording artists must have an association of their own.
17. The recent "Cassette Boom" has adversely affected the number of live programmes and the number of participants for

these programmes.

18. There should be less number of recording companies doing more organised business than more companies doing less organised business.
19. There is a mushroom growth of recording organisations in the country because the organised companies have failed to meet the requirements of the consumers.
20. The artists share equal responsibility with the Industry in fighting against piracy and other unauthorised reproduction of recorded programmes.

21. PLEASE NOTE DOWN YOUR COMMENTS AND SUGGESTIONS.

APPENDIX E

ORGANISATIONS TO WHOM THE QUESTIONNAIRE 1 WAS SENT ACCORDING TO THEIR STATUS AND THE NATURE OF INFORMATION RECEIVED

Sl. No.	Organisation	Place	Status		Questionn-aire		Information		
			IPI	Non-IPI	Ret.	Not ret.	F	P	C
1	2	3	4	5	6	7	8	9	10
1.	The Gramophone Co. of India Ltd.	Calcutta	x		x		x		
2.	Music India Ltd.	Bombay	x			x			
3.	CBS Gramophone Records & Tapes (India) Ltd.	Bombay	x			x			
4.	The Indian Record Mfg. Co. Ltd.	Calcutta	x			x			
5.	Hindustan Musical Products Ltd.	Calcutta	x			x			
6.	The Megaphone Co.	Calcutta	x		x			x	
7.	N.B. Sen & Brothers	Calcutta	x		x		x		
8.	Bharat Records & Musical Products	Calcutta	x			x			
9.	Madan Machinery Mart	Varanasi	x			x			
10.	Gathani Record Co.	Calcutta	x		x				x
11.	Eagle Commercial Co. P. Ltd.	Calcutta	x		x				x
12.	Vijai Radio & Gramophone Co.	Calcutta	x		x				x
13.	SEA Records	Madras	x		x			x	
14.	Deccan Records P. Ltd.	Bangalore	x			x			
15.	Berry Music House	Calcutta	x		x				x
16.	The Master Recording Co.	Madras	x		x		x		
17.	Jyoti Record Mfg. Co. Ltd.	Bombay		x	x		x		

1	2	3	4	5	6	7	8	9	10
18.	Vardhaman Bharati	Bangalore		x	x		x		
19.	Kapco International P. Ltd.	Delhi		x		x			
20.	Amritvani	Hyderabad		x	x		x		
21.	Amritvani	Delhi		x	x		x		
22.	Echo Recording Co.	Madras		x	x		x		
23.	Echo Cassettes & Records	Madras		x	x		x		
24.	AVM Audio	Madras		x	x		x		
25.	Saptaswar	Madras		x	x		x		
26.	A.M. Cassettes	Madras		x	x			x	
27.	Amarnad Cassettes (IBH)	Bombay		x	x			x	
28.	The Oriental Gramophone Records Co.	Bombay		x	x		x		
29.	Sonotone	Delhi		x	x		x		
30	Tharangini Records	Trivandrum		x		x			
31.	Cisons Electronics P. Ltd.	Madras		x		x			
32.	Bani Music Co.	Madras		x		x			
33.	Sirco Cassettes	Madras		x		x			
34.	Vijay Laxmi Music Service	Karnool		x		x			
35.	T. Series Cassettes	Delhi		x		x			
36.	Sai Supra	Madras		x		x			
37.	Idayam Educational Cassettes	Madras		x		x			
38.	Super Hit Music P. Ltd.	Bombay		x		x			
39.	Leisure Sounds	Cuttack		x		x			
40.	Thukral Music Centre	Phagwara		x		x			
41.	Kusadig Recording Co.	Ludhiana		x		x			
42.	Geethanjali Recording Co.	Madras		x	x				x
43.	S. Kalyani Recording Co.	Delhi		x		x			

Number of Questionnaires returned (column 6) : 22 (9 IPI + 13 non-IPI)
Full information (column 8) given by : 13 (3 IPI + 10 non-IPI)
Partial information (column 9) given by : 4 (2 IPI + 2 non-IPI)
Consolidated information (column 10) given by : 5 (4 IPI + 1 non-IPI)
Questionnaires : Ret (Returned); Not Ret (Not Returned)
Information : F (Full); P (Partial); C (Consolidated)

APPENDIX F

INDUSTRY REPRESENTATIVES WHO RESPONDED TO QUESTIONNAIRE 2

Navin N. Daswani, Geethanjali, Madras
Srinivasan, Echo Recording Co., Madras
Prem Mirchandani, Jyoti Record Mfg. Co., Bombay
Vijai Menon, The Oriental Gramophone Record Co., Bombay
Vardhman Bharati, Bangalore
Saptaswar, Madras
Mahesh, Sangeetha (The Master Recording Co.,), Madras
T.R. Viswanathan, Echo Recording Co., Madras
Ramamoorthy , Madras

APPENDIX G

ARTISTS WHO RESPONDED TO QUESTIONNAIRE 3

Vandana Bajpai, New Delhi
Lalit Rao, Delhi
Prabha Atre, Bombay
Simon Augustive Sandhy, Bangalore
N.S. Prasad, Bangalore
Mathew John, Bangalore
Chandrashekhar, Bangalore
A.T. Pillay, Bangalore
Sundermoorthy, Bangalore
Chalapati Rao, Hyderabad
Alka Shanker, New Delhi

APPENDIX H

INDIVIDUALS OR ORGANIZATIONS INTERVIEWED

Organizations or Professional Status	
All India Radio and Broadcasting:	E.S. Isaac, Programme Executive
	A. Dutta, Asstt. Station Director
	Sunil Mehra, Director of Research
	Vasantha Kumari, Director, Programme
	S.K. Sharma, Station Director
Industry Personnel:	Jagadish Sonotone, Delhi
	K.K. Kapoor, Kapco, Delhi
	Babbar, Amritvani, Delhi
	Rajendra Gandhi, Kalyani Recording Co., Delhi
	Subbu Raman, Bombay CBS
	Kukreja, CBS, Delhi
	Anil Bagri, Gramco, Delhi
	James, Grand Music, Music
	Prem Mirchandani, Jyoti Records, Bombay
	Lazarus, Music India, Bombay
	S.P. Sharma, Music India, Bombay
	K.K. Talwar, Vijai Radio and Gramophone Co., Calcutta
	R.N. Ghose. Megaphone, Calcutta
	Surinder, Eagle Commercial Co., Calcutta
	Chatterjee, The Indian Record Mfg. Co. Ltd., Calcutta
	Gathani, Gathani Record Co., Calcutta
	Berry, Berry Music House, Calcutta
Artists:	Vandana Bajpai, New Delhi
	G.N. Joshi, Bombay (NCPA)
	Sulabh Chandra, Bombay (NCPA)
	Sumantha Rao, Bombay (NCPA)
Experts & others:	Narayana Menon, New Delhi
	Ashis Nandi, Delhi
	S. Shidore, Bombay and Calcutta (IPI Secy.)

APPENDIX I

ANALYSIS OF THE 22 ORGANISATIONS INCLUDED IN THIS STUDY

Sl. No.	Organisations	Year of establishment	Business						Operating for Years				Ownership			
			Releases R	Releases C	Sale R	Sale C	Import	Export	Less than 2	2-5	6-10	10 more	Individual	Partnership	Public Ltd.	Private Ltd.
1.	The Gramophone Co. of India Ltd., Calcutta	1901	x	x	x	x	x	x				x			x	
2.	The Megaphone Co., Calcutta	1910	x	x	x	x						x		x		
3.	N.B. Sen & Brothers, Calcutta		x		x							x		x		
4.	Gathani Record Co., Calcutta	1976	x	x	x	x					x			x		
5.	Berry Music House, Calcutta	1976	x	x	x	x					x			x		
6*.	Eagle Commercial Co. P.Ltd., Calcutta	1947	x	x	x	x										x
7*.	Vijai Radio & Gramophone Co., Calcutta	1968	x	x	x	x						x		x		
8.	The Master Recording Co., Madras		x	x	x	x					x			x		
9.	SEA Records, Madras		x	x	x	x					x			x		
10.	The Oriental Gramophone Record Co., Bombay	1974	x	x	x	x	x	x			x		x			

Contd.

Contd.

Sl. No.	Organisations	Year of establishment	Business						Operating for Years				Ownership			
			Releases		Sale		Import	Export	Less than 2	2-5	6-10	10 more	Individual	Partnership	Public Ltd.	Private Ltd.
			R	C	R	C										
11.	Jyoti Record Mfg. Co. Ltd. Bombay	1985	x	x	x	x		x	x			x			x	x
12.	Amritvani, Hyderabad			x		x								x		
13.	Amritvani, Delhi	1974		x		x		x			x					
14.	Sonotone, Delhi	1979	x	x	x	x		x			x		x			
15.	Echo Recording Co., Madras		x	x	x	x		x		x			x			
16.	Echo Cassettes & Records, Madras		x	x	x	x								x		
17.	Vardhaman Bharati	1974	x	x	x	x		x				x	x			
18.	Saptaswar, Madras	1983	x	x	x	x			x							
19.	Geethanjali Recording Co., Madras			x	x	x			x					x		
20.	AVM Audio, Madras		x	x	x	x				x				x		
21.	A.M. Cassettes, Madras			x		x				x			x			
22*.	Amarnad Cassettes (IBH), Bombay															
			17	20	18	20	2	7	3	3	7	6	5	11	2	2

Notes: 6. Eagle Commercial Co. Ltd. Calcutta - have been in trade since 1924 at Lahore (now in Pakistan); were distributors for Columbia

7. Vijai Radio & Gram. Co. Calcutta - existing since about 1910 as Victoria Watch Co. or New Victoria Rec. Co. of Lahore; worked as stockist for the HMV. (details not fully known)

22. Amarnad Cassettes, Bombay - Details not reported.

APPENDIX J

A BRIEF WRITE-UP ABOUT THE GRAMOPHONE COMPANY OF INDIA LIMITED

1. **Organisational Structure**

The Gramophone Company of India (GRAMCO) is a subsidiary of the THORN-EMI Group of U.K. which holds 39 per cent of this Company's shares – rest is held by a number of Govt. financial institutions and public shareholders. The Company is managed by a Board of Directors which includes representatives of THORN-EMI, the M.D. of the Company, representative of the Financial Institutions and a few notable personalities as outside Directors.

2. **Technical Operations**

GRAMCO has fully equipped record manufacturing and cassette production facilities installed in its Calcutta Factory capable of producing approx. 9 million records and 10 million pre-recorded cassettes annually. It has its own recording studios located in the four metro cities (Calcutta, Bombay, Delhi and Madras) and complement of well-trained technical staff to run its technical operations.

3. **Relationship with Artists, Authors, Producers, Public or Films**

The Company has a roster of Artists and Film Producers who are under exclusive contracts with GRAMCO, for a period of time – usually not exceeding three years. Authors and Producers are not usually contracted for a period but for specific individual works which are exclusively used by the Company. Artistes and Film Producers are paid Royalties on the sale of their records/cassettes. Authors and Producers are paid either an agreed flat fee or royalties.

International Music recordings are produced and released by GRAMCO under a Government approved agreement with EMI, the parent Company. Under the agreement, Master tapes and graphics are imported for local production of records and cassettes.

GRAMCO also undertakes Custom pressing orders for several independent local 'labels' who do their own recordings and marketing.

The Company occupies a pre-eminent position in the minds of the Indian people and the creative community. GRAMCO was the first Record Company established in the Far East and has had continuous presence in India for over 80 years. Much before the advent of Radio, gramophones and records made by this Company were popular throughout the country and it has in its treasury artistic works of countless legendary performers and it has helped to preserve and propagate the finest traditions of this performing art, not only for the present generation and the posterity in India but also taken our music to the expatriate Indian and International communities in many parts of the world.

4. A Brief History of this Organisation

4.1 The Gramophone Company of India was established in 1902 as a branch of The Gramophone Company of U.K. Ltd. The first factory was established in 1907 from where it moved to its present location in 1927. It started producing and selling records and gramophones right from its inception. Then from 1936, it started making radios. The factory was modernised in the late '50s for manufacturing long-play records and record-players. Till 1970, GRAMCO was the only record manufacturing Company in India. Till today, it occupies a position of pre-eminence and commands a market share of over 70 per cent on records. Consumer electronic product manufacturing has been almost stopped and substantial capacity for the manufacture of pre-recorded cassettes has been established.

Production and Sales — Figures for the Last Five Years: 1980-85

	Production		Total Sales
Year	Records Units	Cassettes Units	(Rs. Crores)
1980-81	70,69,446	6,42,251	18.91
1981-82	69,39,446	13,46,381	20.43
1982-83	49,72,543	10,90,215	15.93
1983-84	46,75,694	14,28,750	13.70
1984-85	—	45,00,000 (est.)	13.50 (est.)

Note: est = estimates.

The repertoire sales mix constitutes approximately 65 per cent of film music, 30 per cent of non-film music and rest 5 per cent – International music. Non-film music primarily constitutes Hindustani and Carnatic Classical music, Devotional and other light music in Hindi and regional languages and also folk and instrumental music. We have a current catalogue of approximately 5000 records and 2000 cassettes which represents the musical works of the best creative talent, this country has produced. The Company has substantial exports of both Ethnic and International music to U.K., North America, Europe, Africa, Middle East, the Near and the Far East. International records are primarily exported to Hungary, Czechoslovakia, Rumania, i.e. the Iron Curtain countries of East Europe through bilateral Trade Agreements between these countries with India.

The Environment

With the gradual increase in popularity of pre-recorded cassettes, demand for record has been fast eroding. As for pre-recorded cassettes, India is one of the highest pirate infested markets in the world, in as much as 95 per cent of the cassette market is estimated to be commanded by the pirates and only 5 per cent share left to the legitimate music industry. The Copyright Law was amended last year and is now one of the most stringent in the world but in the absence of its enforcement, the environment for the organised music industry remains as difficult as before. The pre-recorded cassette market is estimated to be in the region of 60 million units per annum but almost all of it is in the grip of the pirates. Companies like ours are struggling for survival in this extremely difficult environment.

TABLES

TABLE 1: Places from which the Responses to Questionnaires 1, 2 and 3 were received

Questionnaire	Status	Delhi	Calcutta	Bombay	Madras	Hyderabad	Bangalore	Total
1	IPI	— (-)	7 (10)	— (2)	2 (2)	— (-)	— (2)	9
1	Non-IPI	2	—	2	7	1	1	13
2	Industry	—	—	2	6	—	1	9
3	Artists	3	—	1	—	1	6	11
N responded		5	7	5	15	2	8	42

The figures in parentheses in the first row show the number of IPI organisations existing in that city.

TABLE 2: Releases of Indian Music (Excluding Classical Music) by the IPI Organisations According to Category of Music and Format

	Category of Music																								
	Film Music				Semi-Classical Music				Folk Songs				Devotional Songs				Children Songs and Educational Programmes				Miscellaneous[1]				
Year	A	B	C	Total	A	B	C	Total	A	B	C	Total	A	B	C	Total	A	B	C	Total	A	B	C	Total	Grand Total
1975	71	274	—	345	5	51	—	56	1	53	—	54	11	21	—	32	—	2	—	2	6	44	—	50	539
1976	108	429	—	537	10	79	—	89	2	32	—	34	11	21	—	32	2	2	—	4	13	49	—	62	758
1977	137	807	—	944	31	80	—	111	7	36	—	43	34	98	—	132	3	2	—	5	14	83	—	97	1332
1978	162	655	—	817	15	72	—	87	7	49	—	56	31	101	—	132	2	6	—	8	27	83	—	110	1210
1979	216	629	110	955	24	97	—	121	7	55	—	62	32	81	3	116	5	5	—	10	21	51	—	72	1336
1980	168	705	117	990	33	68	13	114	21	46	2	69	43	45	61	149	2	3	—	5	26	35	6	67	1394
1981	197	501	122	820	24	54	16	94	16	67	6	89	33	41	74	148	1	2	—	3	25	16	9	50	1204
1982	196	456	154	806	22	38	19	79	8	35	15	58	33	23	100	156	1	—	—	1	24	22	21	67	1167
1983	205	307	275	787	26	28	28	82	15	42	15	72	32	33	120	185	1	—	4	5	17	20	40	77	1208
1984	201	371	374	946	31	118	70	219	19	325	24	368	37	8	181	226	2	—	3	5	356	229	505	1090	2854
Total	1661	5134	1152	7947	221	685	146	1052	103	740	62	905	297	472	539	1308	19	22	7	48	529	632	581	1742	13002

Formats: A — 33-1/3 RPM (LP); B — other formats in disc; C — cassettes

1 Miscellaneous category also includes, for 1984, the composite figures (not broken year-wise) given by some companies.

Number of Reporting Organizations: 9

TABLE 3: Releases of Indian Music (Excluding Classical Music) by the non-IPI Organisations According to Category of Music and Format

	Category of Music																								
	Film Music				Semi-Classical Music				Folk Songs				Devotional Songs				Children Songs and Educational Programmes				Miscellaneous[1]				Grand Total
Year	A	B	C	Total	A	B	C	Total	A	B	C	Total	A	B	C	Total	A	B	C	Total	A	B	C	Total	
1975	—	—	—	—	—	—	—	—	—	—	—	—	6	5	4	15	—	—	—	—	—	—	—	—	15
1976	—	—	—	—	—	—	—	—	—	—	—	—	1	3	9	13	—	—	—	—	—	—	—	—	13
1977	—	—	—	—	—	—	1	1	—	—	—	—	1	1	20	22	—	—	—	—	—	—	1	1	24
1978	—	—	—	—	—	—	2	2	—	—	—	—	1	1	15	17	—	—	—	—	—	—	8	8	27
1979	—	—	—	—	—	—	—	—	—	1	6	7	1	1	45	47	—	—	1	1	—	—	3	3	58
1980	—	—	—	—	—	—	3	3	—	4	12	16	—	1	80	81	—	—	1	1	—	—	7	7	108
1981	1	4	—	5	—	—	10	10	—	3	28	31	—	1	130	131	—	—	2	2	—	—	6	6	185
1982	14	25	2	41	—	—	20	20	—	2	28	30	1	—	114	115	—	—	12	12	—	—	20	20	238
1983	36	146	49	231	15	—	68	83	—	2	25	27	—	3	129	132	—	—	24	24	—	—	43	43	540
1984	80	296	81	457	18	—	91	109	2	2	32	36	19	7	129	155	—	—	27	27	9	—	22	31	815
Total	131	471	132	734	33	—	195	228	2	14	131	147	30	23	675	728	—	—	67	67	9	—	110	119	2023

Formats: A — 33-1/3 RPM (LP); B — other formats in disc; C — cassettes

[1] Miscellaneous category also includes, for 1984, the composite figures (not broken year-wise) given by some companies.

Number of Reporting Organizations: 13

TABLE 4: Releases of Indian Music (Excluding Classical Music) by all the Respondent Organisations by Category of Music and Formats

Year	Film Music				Semi-Classical Music				Folk Songs				Devotional Songs				Children Songs Educational Programmes				Miscellaneous[1]				Grand Total
	A	B	C	Total	A	B	C	Total	A	B	C	Total	A	B	C	Total	A	B	C	Total	A	B	C	Total	
1975	71	274	—	345	5	51	—	56	1	53	—	54	17	26	4	47	—	2	—	2	6	44	—	50	554
1976	108	429	—	537	10	79	—	89	2	32	—	34	12	24	9	45	2	2	—	4	13	49	—	62	771
1977	137	807	—	944	31	80	1	112	7	36	—	43	35	99	20	154	3	2	—	5	14	83	1	98	1356
1978	162	655	—	817	15	72	2	89	7	49	—	56	32	102	15	149	2	6	—	8	27	83	8	118	1237
1979	216	629	110	955	24	97	—	121	7	56	6	69	33	82	48	163	5	5	1	11	21	51	3	75	1394
1980	168	705	117	990	33	68	16	117	21	50	14	85	43	46	141	230	2	3	1	6	26	35	13	74	1502
1981	198	505	122	825	24	54	26	104	16	70	34	120	33	42	204	279	1	2	2	5	25	16	15	56	1389
1982	210	481	156	847	22	38	39	99	8	37	43	88	34	23	214	271	1	—	12	13	24	22	41	87	1405
1983	241	453	324	1018	41	28	96	165	15	44	40	99	32	36	249	317	1	—	28	29	17	20	83	120	1748
1984	281	667	455	1403	49	118	161	328	21	327	56	404	56	15	310	381	2	—	30	32	365	229	527	1121	3669
Total	1792	5605	1284	8681	254	685	341	1280	105	754	197	1052	327	495	1214	2036	19	22	74	115	538	632	691	1861	15025

Formats: A — 33-1/3 RPM (LP); B — other formats in disc; C — cassettes

[1] Miscellaneous category also includes, for 1984, the composite figures (not broken year-wise) given by some companies.

Number of Reporting Organizations: 22 (IPI-9; non-IPI-13).

TABLE 5: Number of Releases According to Languages[1]

Year		Languages														
		Hindi	Gujarati	Marathi	Punjabi	Rajas-thani	Bengali	Assamese	Oriya	Tamil	Telugu	Mala-yalam	Kannada	Urdu	Other Languages	Total
1975	N	40	40	38	68	9	60	6	3	—	—	—	—	38	11	313
	%	12.77	12.77	12.10	21.72	2.88	19.17	1.92	0.96					12.10	3.51	
1976	N	230	78	40	58	3	62	10	18	—	2	—	—	40	21	562
	%	40.92	13.88	7.12	10.32	0.53	11.03	1.78	3.20		0.36			7.12	3.74	
1977	N	290	57	41	50	7	164	12	29	194	184	157	93	37	17	1332
	%	21.77	4.28	3.08	3.75	0.53	12.31	0.90	2.18	14.56	13.81	11.79	6.98	2.78	1.28	
1978	N	228	38	14	78	6	149	19	29	184	203	123	74	36	22	1203
	%	18.95	3.16	1.16	6.48	0.50	12.38	1.58	2.41	15.30	16.87	10.22	6.15	2.99	1.83	
1979	N	273	37	35	73	8	128	28	17	192	273	109	55	46	13	1287
	%	21.21	2.87	2.72	5.67	0.62	9.94	2.18	1.32	14.92	21.21	8.47	4.27	3.57	1.01	
1980	N	387	43	34	114	11	107	10	24	196	254	88	97	34	18	1417
	%	27.31	3.03	2.40	8.04	0.78	7.55	0.70	1.69	13.83	17.92	6.21	6.84	2.40	1.27	
1981	N	295	43	70	130	13	99	11	21	145	153	87	241	30	37	1375
	%	21.45	3.13	5.09	9.45	0.94	0.72	0.08	1.53	10.54	11.13	6.33	17.53	2.18	2.69	
1982	N	335	37	48	129	7	91	12	15	999	165	95	176	37	40	2186
	%	15.32	1.69	2.20	5.90	0.32	4.16	0.55	0.67	45.70	7.55	4.34	8.05	1.69	1.83	
1983	N	341	34	42	119	5	118	11	12	221	157	149	137	42	38	1426
	%	23.91	2.38	2.94	8.34	0.35	8.27	0.77	0.84	15.49	11.00	10.45	9.61	2.94	2.66	
1984	N	362	56	63	80	3	158	28	6	321	236	104	169	65	53	1704
	%	21.44	3.29	3.70	4.69	0.18	9.27	1.64	0.35	18.84	13.85	6.10	9.92	3.81	3.11	
Total	N	2781	463	425	899	72	1136	147	174	2452	1627	912	1042	405	270	12805
	%	21.71	3.62	3.32	7.02	0.56	8.87	1.15	1.36	19.15	12.71	7.12	8.14	3.16	2.11	

[1] Data received in composite figures for different languages has been excluded;
Blank cells (—) mean that data were not reported;
Number of Reporting Organisations: 22.
% is the proportion of the row Total (reported in the last column), i.e. the total number of releases during that year.

TABLE 6: Distribution of Releases According to the Categories of Music (Excluding Classical Music), Arranged According to Languages

Category of music		Hindi	Gujarati	Mara-thi	Punjabi	Rajas-thani	Bengali	Assa-mese	Oriya	Tamil	Telugu	Mala-yalam	Kan-nada	Urdu	Other Languages	Total
		Languages														
Film Songs	N	2653	314	223	140	—	354	62	74	1118	1397	704	679	—	3	7721
	%	34.36	4.07	2.89	1.81		4.58	0.80	0.96	14.48	18.09	9.12	8.79		0.04	
Semi-Classical Music	N	84	15	62	24	3	321	30	63	—	—	—	—	597	28	1227
	%	6.84	1.22	5.05	1.96	0.24	26.16	2.44	5.13					48.66	2.28	
Folk Songs	N	73	29	34	341	47	77	20	5	1	6	2	7	—	90	732
	%	9.97	3.96	4.64	46.60	6.42	10.52	2.73	0.68	0.14	0.82	0.27	0.96		12.30	
Devotional Songs	N	243	68	65	356	8	41	1	24	421	131	45	181	4	76	1664
	%	14.60	4.09	3.91	21.39	0.46	2.46	0.06	1.44	25.30	7.87	2.70	10.88	0.24	4.57	
Children's Songs and Educational Programmes	N	21	6	9	5	—	12	1	—	1	2	—	1	—	6	64
	%	32.81	9.38	14.06	7.81		18.75	1.56		1.56	3.12		1.56		9.38	
Miscellaneous	N	107	29	32	37	13	369	34	8	51	93	12	27	4	83	899
	%	11.90	3.22	3.56	4.12	1.45	41.04	3.78	0.89	5.67	10.34	1.33	3.00	0.44	9.23	
Total	N	3181	461	425	903	71	1174	148	174	1592	1629	763	895	605	286	12307
	%	25.85	3.74	3.45	7.34	0.58	9.54	1.20	1.41	12.94	13.24	6.20	7.27	4.92	2.32	

Number of Reporting Organisations: 22.
% is the proportion of the row Total (reported in the last column), i.e. the total number of releases during that year.
Blank cells (—) mean that data were not reported.

TABLE 7: Distribution of Releases According to the Language of Recording Arranged According to Categories of Music (Excludin Classical Music)

Category of music		Hindi	Gujarati	Marathi	Punjabi	Rajasthani	Bengali	Assamese	Oriya	Tamil	Telugu	Malayalam	Kannada	Urdu	Other Languages	Total
		Languages														
Film Songs	N	2653	314	223	140	—	354	62	74	1118	1397	704	679	—	3	7721
	%	83.40	68.11	52.47	15.50		30.15	41.89	42.53	70.23	85.76	92.27	75.86		1.05	62.73
Semi-Classical Music	N	84	15	62	24	3	321	30	63	—	—	—	—	597	28	1227
	%	2.64	3.25	14.59	2.66	4.22	27.34	20.27	36.21					98.68	9.79	9.97
Folk Songs	N	73	29	34	341	47	77	20	5	1	6	2	7	—	90	732
	%	2.29	6.29	8.00	37.76	66.20	6.56	13.51	2.87	0.06	0.37	0.26	0.78		31.47	5.95
Devotional Songs	N	243	68	65	356	8	41	1	240	421	131	45	181	4	76	1664
	%	7.64	14.75	15.29	39.42	11.27	3.49	0.68	13.79	26.44	8.04	5.90	20.22	0.66	26.57	13.52
Children's Songs and Educational Programmes	N	21	6	9	5	—	12	1	—	1	2	—	1	—	6	64
	%	0.66	1.30	2.12	0.55		1.02	0.68		0.06	0.12		0.11		2.10	0.52
Miscellaneous	N	107	29	32	37	13	369	34	8	51	93	12	27	4	83	899
	%	3.36	6.29	7.53	4.10	18.31	31.43	22.97	4.60	3.20	5.71	1.57	3.01	0.66	29.02	7.30
Total		3181	461	425	903	71	1174	148	174	1592	1629	763	895	605	286	12307

Blank cells (—) mean that data were not reported or reported as nil.
Number of Reporting Organizations: 22.
% is the proportion of the Column Total, reported in the bottom line i.e. the total number of releases for that language.

TABLE 8: Share of IPI and non-IPI Organisations in the Total Number of Releases (Excluding Classical Music)

Year	IPI		Non-IPI		Row Total
	N	%	N	%	
1975	539	97.30	15	2.70	554
1976	758	98.31	13	1.69	771
1977	1332	98.23	24	1.77	1356
1978	1210	97.82	27	2.18	1237
1979	1336	95.84	58	4.16	1394
1980	1394	92.81	108	7.19	1502
1981	1204	86.68	185	13.32	1389
1982	1167	83.06	238	16.94	1405
1983	1208	69.11	540	30.89	1748
1984	2854	77.79	815	22.21	3669
Total	13002	86.54	2023	13.46	15025

N = actual number of releases. % = proportion of the row total.
Number of Reporting Organizations: 22 (IPI- 9, non-IPI-13).

TABLE 9: Share of IPI and non-IPI Respondents in the Total Number of Releases (Excluding Classical Music), According to the Categories of Music

Year		Film Music			Semi-Classical Music			Folk Songs			Devotional Songs			Children Songs Educational Programmes			Miscellaneous			Grand Total
		IPI	Non-IPI	Total	IPI	Non-IPI	Total	IPI	Non-IPI	Total	IPI	Non-IPI	Total	IPI	Non-IPI	Total	IPI	Non-IPI	Total	
1975	N	345	—	345	56	—	56	54	—	54	32	15	47	2	—	2	50	—	50	554
	%	100.0	—		100.0	—		100.0	—		68.09	31.91		100.0			100.0	—		
1976	N	537	—	537	89	—	89	34	—	34	32	13	45	4	—	4	62	—	62	771
	%	100.0	—		100.0	—		100.0	—		71.11	28.89		100.0	—		100.0	—		
1977	N	944	—	944	111	1	112	43	—	43	132	22	154	5	—	5	97	1	98	1356
	%	100.0	—		99.11	0.9		100.0	—		71.11	14.29		100.0	—		98.98	1.02		
1978	N	817	—	817	87	2	89	56	—	56	132	17	149	8	—	8	110	8	118	1237
	%	100	—		97.75	2.25		100	—		88.59	11.41		100.0	—		93.22	6.78		
1979	N	955	—	955	121	—	121	62	7	69	116	47	163	10	1	11	72	3	75	1394
	%	100.0	—		100.0	—		89.86	10.14		71.17	28.84		90.91	9.09		96.00	4.00		
1980	N	990	—	990	114	3	117	69	16	85	149	81	230	5	1	6	67	7	74	1502
	%	100.0	—		97.44	2.56		81.18	18.82		64.78	35.22		83.33	16.67		90.54	9.46		
1981	N	820	5	825	94	10	104	89	31	120	148	131	279	3	2	5	50	6	56	1389
	%	99.40	0.60		90.39	9.61		74.17	25.83		53.05	46.95		60.00	40.00		89.28	10.72		
1982	N	806	41	847	79	20	99	58	30	88	156	115	271	1	12	13	67	20	87	1405
	%	95.16	4.84		79.80	20.20		65.91	34.09		57.56	42.44		7.69	92.31		77.01	22.99		
1983	N	787	231	1018	82	83	165	72	27	99	185	132	317	5	24	29	77	43	120	1748
	%	77.31	22.69		49.70	50.30		72.73	27.27		58.36	41.64		17.24	82.76		64.17	35.83		
1984	N	946	457	1403	219	109	328	368	36	404	226	155	381	5	27	32	1090	31	1121	3669
	%	67.43	32.57		66.77	33.23		90.20	8.82		59.32	40.68		15.62	84.38		97.23	2.77		
Total	N	7947	734	8681	1052	228	1280	905	147	1052	1308	728	2036	48	67	115	1742	119	1861	15025
	%	91.54	8.46		82.19	17.81		85.70	13.92		64.34	35.76		41.74	58.26		93.60	6.40		

N = actual number of releases
% is the proportion of the Row Total (reported in the last column), i.e. the total number of releases during that year.

TABLE 10: Proportion of Total Releases (Excluding Classical Music) Arranged According to the Categories of Music

Year		Categories of Music						
		Film	Semi-Classical	Folk	Devotional	Children's & Educ. Programmes	Miscellaneous	Total
1975	N	345	56	54	47	2	50	554
	%	62.27	10.11	9.75	8.48	0.36	9.02	
1976	N	537	89	34	45	4	62	771
	%	69.65	11.54	4.41	5.84	0.52	8.04	
1977	N	944	112	43	154	5	98	1356
	%	69.62	8.26	3.18	11.36	0.37	7.23	
1978	N	817	89	56	149	8	118	1237
	%	66.05	7.19	4.53	12.04	0.65	9.54	
1979	N	955	121	69	163	11	75	1394
	%	68.51	8.68	4.95	11.69	0.79	5.38	
1980	N	990	117	85	230	6	74	1502
	%	65.91	7.79	5.66	15.31	0.40	4.93	
1981	N	825	104	120	279	5	56	1389
	%	59.40	7.49	8.64	20.09	0.36	4.03	
1982	N	847	99	88	271	13	87	1405
	%	60.28	7.05	6.26	19.29	0.92	6.19	
1983	N	1018	165	99	317	29	120	1748
	%	58.24	9.44	5.66	18.13	1.66	8.86	
1984	N	1403	328	404	381	32	1121	3669
	%	38.24	8.94	11.07	10.38	0.87	30.56	
Total	N	8681	1280	1052	2036	115	1861	15025
	%	57.78	8.52	7.00	13.55	0.76	12.39	

N = actual number of releases
Number of Reporting Organisations. 22 (IPI-9, non-IPI-13).
% is the proportion of the row total reported in the last column, i.e. the total number of releases during that year.

TABLE 11: Releases of Indian Classical Music[1]

	Hindustani Music (North Indian)					Carnatic Music (South Indian)					
	Vocal 1		Instru-mental 2		3 Total	Vocal 4		Instru-mental 5		6 Total	Grand Total
Year	R	C	R	C	(1+2)	R	C	R	C	(4+5)	(3+6)
1975	5	—	12	—	17	—	—	—[2]	—[2]	—	17
1976	9	—	4	—	13	—	—	—[2]	—[2]	—	13
1977	9	—	4	—	13	—	—	11	—	11	24
1978	3	—	11	1	15	—	—	7	—	7	22
1979	10	—	4	2	16	—	—	10	—	10	26
1980	11	—	18	13	42	—	4	11	11	26	68
1981	7	5	8	15	35	—	10	9	23	42	77
1982	2	9	5	23	39	—	7	—	12	19	58
1983	8	16	22	30	76	11	20	18	42	91	167
1984	6	18	10	16	50	10	60	15	59	144	194
Total	70	48	98	100	316	21	101	81	147	350	666
C[3]	—	2	—	6	8	—	—	—	—	—	8
Grand Total	70	50	98	106	324	21	101	81	147	350	674

R — Records C — Cassettes

1 This is a consolidated table for both IPI and non-IPI organizations. The contribution of the non-IPI members is considerably small and hence not given in a separate table. Even in this, the share of GRAMCO is highest, far exceeding the others especially in Records. It is after 1980 that a substantial no. of cassettes by other organizations, appeared especially in Carnatic music. However, GRAMCO remains the largest producer organizations in the total release of classical music.

2 Figures not reported: reported as 'figures not available'.

3 This is an additional consolidated figures given by a company for the entire 10-year period.

Number of Reporting Organizations — 10 (3 IPI + 7 non-IPI).

TABLE 12: Releases of Indian Classical Music: Contributions Made by GRAMCO and other Organisations during the Ten-Year Period

		Hindustani Music (North Indian)					Carnatic Music (South Indian)					
		1 Vocal		2 Instrumental		3 Total (1+2)	4 Vocal		5 Instrumental		6 Total (4+5)	Grand Total (3+6)
Organisation	N*	R	C	R	C		R	C	R	C		
GRAMCO	1	69	23	98	51	241	–	–	60	59	119	360
Other IPIs	2	1	3	–	9	13	1	41	–	48	90	103
Non-IPIs	7	–	24	–	46	70	20	60	21	40	141	211
Total	10	70	50	98	106	324	21	101	81	147	350	674

N* — Number of organizations represented in the category.
R — Records; C — Cassettes

TABLE 13-A: Production: Units of Records and Cassettes Produced by an IPI Member — GRAMCO — According to the Category of Music
(Figures in thousands)

Year	Film R	Film C	Classical R	Classical C	Semi-Classical R	Semi-Classical C	Others[1] R	Others[1] C	International R	International C	Total R	Total C	Grand Total
1975	3535	—	292	—	58	—	1187	—	771	—	5843	—	5843
1976	3997	—	356	—	65	—	1261	—	789	—	6468	—	6468
1977	4606	—	435	—	145	—	1305	—	762	—	7253	—	7253
1978	5199	—	487	—	260	—	1430	—	739	—	8115	—	8115
1979	4134	—	384	—	251	—	1323	—	529	—	6621	—	6621
1980	4224	388	379	36	281	88	1614	52	512	43	7010	607	7617
1981	3883	611	329	79	263	249	1646	113	461	79	6582	1131	7713
1982	2829	614	251	82	190	179	1218	92	251	56	4739	1023	5762
1983	2450	807	221	130	161	259	1024	173	161	72	4017	1441	5458
1984	1910	1706	183	274	120	518	823	396	127	152	3163	3046	6209
Total	36767	4126	3317	601	1794	1293	12831	826	5102	402	59811	7248	67059
Total R + C	40893		3918		3087		13657		5504		67059		
%[2]	60.98		5.84		4.60		20.37		8.21				

[1] 'Others' Category here includes folk, children's and educational, devotional and miscellaneous songs.

R — Records C — Cassettes

[2] Proportion of the total combined production of Records and Cassettes-67059-expressed in percentages.

TABLE 13-B: Production: Units of Records and Cassettes Produced by an IPI Member — The Master Recording Co., Madras — According to the Category of Music

(Figures in thousands)

	Category of Music																	
	Film		Classical		Semi Classical		Folk		Devotional		Children's Educational Programmes		Miscella-neous		Internation-al		Total	
Year	R	C	R	C	R	C	R	C	R	C	R	C	R	C	R	C	R	C
1975	—	—	—	—	—	—	—	—	—	—	—	—	—	—	—	—	—	—
1976	—	—	—	—	—	—	—	—	—	—	—	—	—	—	—	—	—	—
1977	—	—	—	—	—	—	—	—	—	—	—	—	—	—	—	—	—	—
1978	—	—	—	—	—	—	—	—	—	—	—	—	—	—	—	—	—	—
1979	—	—	—	—	—	—	—	—	—	—	—	—	—	—	—	—	—	—
1980	—	8	—	—	—	—	—	—	—	15	—	—	—	2	—	—	—	25
1981	—	25	—	—	—	—	—	6	—	82	—	—	—	10	—	—	—	123
1982	—	22	—	—	—	—	—	2	—	45	—	—	—	13	—	—	—	82
1983	—	25	—	—	—	—	—	5	—	46	—	2	—	8	—	—	—	86
1984	—	39	—	—	—	—	—	9	—	59	—	—	—	9	—	—	—	116
Total	—	119	—	—	—	—	—	22	—	247	—	2	—	42	—	—	—	432
%[1]	—	27.55	—	—	—	—	—	5.10	—	57.18	—	0.46	—	9.72	—	—	—	

R — Records C — Cassettes

[1] Proportion of the total production-432-expressed in percentages.

TABLE 13-C: Production: Units of Records and Cassettes Produced by 8 non-IPI Members According to the Category of Music

(Figures in thousands)

	Category of Music																		
	Film		Classical		Semi-Classical		Folk		Devotional		Children's Educational Programmes		Miscellaneous		International		Total		Grand Total
Year	R	C	R	C	R	C	R	C	R	C	R	C	R	C	R	C	R	C	
1975	—	—	—	—	—	—	—	—	—	—	—	—	—	—	—	—	—	—	—
1976	—	—	—	—	—	—	—	0.1	—	0.1	—	—	—	—	—	—	—	0.2	0.2
1977	—	—	—	—	—	—	—	—	—	0.1	—	—	—	0.1	—	—	—	0.2	0.2
1978	—	—	—	—	—	—	—	—	—	17.2	—	—	—	0.3	—	—	—	17.5	17.5
1979	—	—	—	—	—	—	—	1	—	35.0	—	—	—	0.5	—	—	—	36.5	36.5
1980	—	—	—	—	—	—	—	6	—	43.0	—	—	—	0.5	—	—	—	49.5	49.5
1981	5.3	2.75	—	—	—	—	—	4	—	44.0	—	—	—	0.5	—	—	5.3	51.25	56.55
1982	89.5	23.7	—	—	—	—	—	5	13.4	41.6	—	3	—	2.6	—	—	102.9	75.9	178.8
1983	139.0	23.6	5	2	—	—	—	4	17.3	41.0	—	4	5	12.6	—	—	166.3	87.2	253.5
1984	246.1	93.5	5	2	6	23	—	4	30.7	60.4	—	—	10	24.0	—	—	297.8	206.9	504.7
Total	479.9	143.55	10	4	6	23	—	24.1	61.4	282.4	—	7	15	41.1	—	—	572.3	525.15	1097.45
Total R+C	623.45		14		29		24.1		343.8		7		56.1		-		1097.45		1097.45
%[1]	56.81		1.28		2.64		2.20		31.32		0.64		5.11		—				

R — Records C — Cassettes

[1] Proportions of the Total Production — 1097.45 thousands — expressed in percentages.

TABLE 14: Sale: Units of Records and Cassettes Sold

(Figures in thousands)

	IPI Organizations			Non-IPI Organizations			Total		Grand Total
Year	R	C	Total	R	C	Total	R	C	(R + C)
1975	4882	—	4882	0.9	0.6	1.5	4882.9	0.6	4883.5
1976	5431	—	5431	0.1	0.7	0.8	5431.1	0.7	5431.8
1977	5983	—	5983	0.75	0.5	1.25	5983.75	0.5	5984.25
1978	7693	47	7740	0.2	86	86.2	7693.2	133	7826.2
1979	6660	195	6855	0.05	116.1	116.15	6660.05	311.1	6971.15
1980	6953.6	577	7530.6	0.1	129.2	129.3	6953.7	706.2	7659.9
1981	6925	1217	8142	0.85	153	153.85	6925.85	1370	8295.85
1982	4651.6	966	5617.6	81.75	231.9	313.65	4733.35	1197.9	5931.25
1983	3990.2	1555	5545.2	168.51	228.75	397.26	4158.71	1783.75	5942.46
1984	2699.2	3760	6459.2	263.95	282.5	546.45	2963.15	4042.5	7005.65
Total	55868.6	8317	64185.6	517.16	1229.25	1746.41	56385.76	9546.25	65932.01
%[1]	87.04	12.96		29.61	70.39		85.52	14.48	

R — Records C — Cassettes

[1] Proportions of the Total Sales of Records and Cassettes expressed in percentages, separately for IPI and non-IPI organisations, and for the Total Sales reported in the last column.

Number of reporting organizations: 14 (IPI — 5, non-IPI — 9).

TABLE 15: Import: Units of Masters Imported by One non-IPI Organisation

	Year										
	1975	1976	1977	1978	1979	1980	1981	1982	1983	1984	Total
Units Imported	—	—	—	—	48	24	—	24	—	6	102

TABLE 16-A: Exports of Records and Cassettes reported by the GRAMCO, showing the countries where exported

(Figures in thousands)

	Year																						
	1975[a]		1976[b]		1977		1978		1979		1980		1981		1982		1983		1984		Total		Grand Total
Country	R	C	R	C	R	C	R	C	R	C	R	C	R	C	R	C	R	C	R	C	R	C	
UK					360	—	244	35	154	60	122	40	146	79	157	43	119	37	82	56	1384	350	1734
West Europe					56	—	127	4	75	3	77	2	37	—	—	—	27	—	28	—	427	9	436
North America					114	—	138	5	108	3	150	5	138	19	74	16	86	20	71	17	879	85	964
South America					113	—	75	3	91	2	68	—	46	—	30	2	13	2	7	—	443	9	452
West Asia					57	—	69	1	34	27	17	29	19	20	13	9	5	4	2	3	216	93	309
Africa					22	—	36	—	8	1	12	2	5	—	3	—	2	—	1	—	89	3	92
South East Asia					7	—	10	—	16	1	18	—	6	2	5	—	11	—	2	—	75	3	78
Far East					40	—	49	—	53	7	56	11	40	14	11	3	10	—	9	3	268	38	306
Australia					21	—	17	3	21	22	18	24	15	11	8	6	6	5	4	1	110	72	182
Total[a]	615	—	654	—	790	—	765	51	560	126	538	113	452	145	301	79	279	68	206	80	5160[c]	662	5822[c]
East Europe[b]	346	26	384	10	481	10	465	17	493	4	529	43	605	93	486	33	251	68	463	18	4503	322	4825
Grand Total	961	26	1038	10	1271	10	1230	68	1053	130	1067	156	1057	238	787	112	530	136	669	98	9663	984	10647

R — Records C — Cassettes

[a] 1975 and 1976 break-up not available

[b] East Europe exports are of International music. For other countries, Indian music of all categories.

[c] Row total: The total exceeds the column totals of records by 1269 Records because of the extra total exports of 615 and 654 records in 1975 and 1976 respectively (shown without country break-up).

TABLE 16-B: Contributions of 5 Reporting Organizations in Total Exports

(Figures in thousands)

Exported to	1975		1976		1977		1978		1979		1980		1981		1982		1983		1984		Total		Grand Total
	R	C	R	C	R	C	R	C	R	C	R	C	R	C	R	C	R	C	R	C	R	C	
A	961	26	1038	10	1271	10	1230	68	1053	130	1067	156	1057	238	787	112	530	136	669	98	9663	984	10647
B	—	—	—	—	—	—	—	—	—	—	—	—	—	—	—	—	—	—	—	25	—	25	25
C	—	—	—	—	—	—	—	—	—	—	—	—	—	—	—	—	—	—	1	—	1	—	1
D	—	—	—	—	—	—	—	—	—	—	13	25	7	18	2	5	1	15	14	45	37	108	145
E	—	—	—	—	—	—	—	—	—	—	—	—	—	3	—	5	—	5	—	3	—	16	16
Total	961	26	1038	10	1271	10	1230	68	1053	130	1080	181	1064	259	789	122	531	156	684	171	9701	1133	10834

R — Records C — Cassettes

Explanation:

A — Exports to U.K., West Indies, North America, South America, West Asia, Africa, South-east Asia, Far East, Australia and East Europe (same as in Table 16-A). ; includes International and Indian music.

B — Exports to U.K.

C — Exports to U.K.; U.S.A.; Belgium.

D — Exports to Africa; U.S.A.; Indian music

E — Exports to U.K.

B, C, and E have filled in for International music but we suspect it is Indian music. It has to be verified.

TABLE 17-A: Responses to the Questionnaire 2: How the Industry Perceives Itself and Other Related Matters

Motivational urges and general outlook

(Questions : 2-9)

Q	R	N	F
2.	How do you feel being in the industry?	6	
	— happy		4
	— happy but suffering		1
	— thriving		1
3.	Do you think the industry is growing or retarding?	8	
	— growing		6
	— growing and retarding		1
	— growing in an unhealthy way		1
4.	What are the negative trends in the industry?	6	
	— bad attitudes of top singers (not allowing smaller to come-up)		1
	— non-availability of quality tapes		1
	— piracy		5
	— lack of cooperation among industry market		1
5.	What are the positive trends in the industry?	6	
	— awakening among producers		1
	— opportunity to new singers		1
	— growing interest in Indian music and culture		1
	— purchasing capacity increased		1
	— basic 'Records' still sell		1
	— popularity of film music		1
	— growing consumer interest		2
	— promoting cultural programmes		1
	— popularity of electronic equipment		1
	— industry is picking up now		1
6.	What do you think is the goals of the phonographic industry?	6	
	a. Primary goal		
	— promotion of artistic values		1
	— entertain		1
	— educate		1
	— elevate		1
	— eradicate piracy		1
	— catering to customers' taste		1
	— earning money, and profit		2

b. Secondary goal	2	
— earning		1
— encouraging new artists		1
— promotion of culture		1
7. What do you think about the role of phonogram in cultural communication?	4	
— tremendous and important		2
— entertainment		1
— cross-cultural programmes and understanding		1
— develop cultural activities		1
8. What role does the industry play in the development of culture in India?	3	
— degrading the Indian culture		1
— sustaining the development		1
— keeping alive the traditional music		1
— promoting, spreading masters (music-creators)		1
9. Does your company have a cultural policy of its own? If yes, explain the policy	6	
— raise human values		1
— give the customers what he wants		1
— promoting classical and devotional music		2
— encouraging the new talent		1
— recording old masters		1
— folklore		1
— ancient culture		1
— East and West re-alignment		1
— not specially		1
— promoting regional music		1

Note: Question (Q) followed by responses (R), the no. of respondents to that question (N) and frequency of the response (F).

TABLE 17-B: Responses to the Questionnaire 2 : How the Industry Perceives Itself and Other Related Matters

Recording Industry and the Government

(Questions : 10-12)

Q	R	N	F
10.	Are you satisfied with the cultural policy of the Government with regard to the industry? If not, what changes would you like to have?	9	
a.	– satisfied		2
	– not satisfied		2
b.	changes needed		
	– immediate check on piracy		4
	– no interference		1
	– remove excise duty		2
	– other taxation reforms		2
	– permission to be given to import tapes and master tapes to the licensed companies		1
	– check unlicensed expansion		1
	– encourage more licensed trade; competition to beat piracy		1
	– study AIR's role in catering to the people's needs		1
11.	Do you think there is a general lack of awareness about the recording industry among Government departments	6	
	– yes		5
	– no		1
	(not informed of piracy)		
12.	Do you think the Government considers the phonogram as important a medium as film, books etc. for cultural communication?	7	
	– yes		2
	– no		5

Note: Question (Q) followed by responses (R), the no. of respondents to that question (N) and frequency of the response (F).

TABLE 17-C: Responses to the Questionnaire 2 : How the Industry Perceives Itself and Other Related Matters

Relationship with Artists, Producers etc.

(Questions 13-18)

Q	R	N	F
13.	Do you think the artists/producers are satisfied with the industry	6	
	— satisfied		
	yes		3
	no		3
	— reasons for satisfaction		
	royalty		4
	prestige		2
	creditability		1
	personal relationship		3
	any other		
	— 'missionary motive of our ideology'		
	— 'Dissatisfaction in royalty payments'		
14.	Do you think there is scope for improving the relationship? How?	3	
	— yes		3
	— mutual respects and looking after artists generally		
	— prompt royalty		
15.	Do you think the industry should have uniform policy on royalty?	8	
	— yes		6
	— no		2
16.	Do you think royalty rates should be same for all artists irrespective of their popularity and social prestige?	7	
	— yes		3
	— no		4
17.	Do you think the policy of exclusive contracts needs to be reviewed? If yes, give reasons?	6	
	— yes		3
	— for otherwise the artists will be exploited or neglected		
	— no		3
18.	Do you have any suggestions on the system of contracts?		
	— speedy Governmental action to check		
	— free system		
	— contracting for a lesser period — say one year		

Note: Question (Q) followed by responses (R), the no. of respondents to that questions (N) and frequency giving that response (F).

TABLE 17-D: Responses to the Questionnaire 2 : How the Industry Perceives Itself and Other Related Matters

Copyright

(Questions — 19-23)

Q	R	N	F
19.	What do you think about the Copyright Amendment Act of October 1984? Is it an effective one?	6	
	— effective		2
	— not effective		4
20.	Do you think it has been effectively implemented?		
	— yes		1
	— no		5
21.	What are the problems in the implementation of this Act?		
	— not proper understanding by authors		9
	— no proper circulation		9
	— inpractibility and expansiveness in cost and legal expenses		7
	— it has to be done gradually in stages		6
22.	What is the role to be played by the Government in this regard?	2	
	— empower the artist, industries and authorities with more powers		7
	— take more effective steps		6
	— seize pirated material at source, at shops etc. and fine the sellers		3
	— no control; not implemented		2
23.	What is the role to be played by the industry in this regard?	3	
	— mutual cooperation		7
	— coordination		6
	— Union (with universal) membership		3
	— legal side still weak		1

Note: Question (Q) followed by responses (R), the no. of respondents to the questions (N) and frequency giving that response (F)

TABLE 17-E: Responses to the Questionnaire 2 : How the Industry Perceives Itself and Other Related Matters

Import-Export

(Questions 24-29)

Only one respondent answered as under:

Q	R

24. How does the Government policy affect import and export of phonograms?
    — quality tapes are not available through Government. They should be easily provided to the organizations.

25. What changes would you wish in the import-export policy of the Indian Government?
    — easy import and speedy export without too much formalities

26. What type of music do you import: more of serious music or pop music? Why?
    — we do not import any type of music

27. What type of music you export: more of Indian music or International music? Why?
    — Indian music only, to spread and propagate its sublining, elevating, tranquil qualities and capabilities

28. What are the guiding factors for other countries for importing phonograms from India? Specify?
    (a) Economic reasons
    (b) Political Reasons
    (c) Cultural Reasons — All the three, more the cultural

29. Do you think there is a growing interest in Indian music among foreigners? Substantiate your answer with data if possible?
    — Yes, we have noticed this during our three programme tours abroad and interest envinced in our cassettes.

Note: Question (Q) followed by responses (R).

TABLE 17-F: Responses to the Questionnaire 2 : How the Industry Perceives Itself and Other Related Matters

Problems facing the industry

(Questions 30-32)

Q	R	N	F
30.	What are the most important problems facing the industry today?	8	
	— piracy		8
	— paucity of tapes		1
	— non-availability of quality tapes		2
31.	What are your suggestions to tackle each of these problems?	6	
	— strict Govt. policy for speedy punishment of pirates		1
	— quality control over tapes and goods		2
	strict implementation		1
	— relaxation of rigid rules of import & manufacture		2
	— create fear among pirates		1
32.	Do you think the public is aware of these problems? If not, what you think is to be done.	3	
	— yes		1
	— no		3

Note: Question (Q) followed by responses (R), the no. of respondents to that question (N) and frequency giving that response (F).

TABLE 17-G: Responses in the Questionaire2: How the Industry Perceives Itself and Other Related Matters

Future of Recording Industry

(Question 33-34)

Q	R	N	F
33.	What do you think is the future of the recording industry?	8	
	— bright		8
34.	What do you think are the future challenges to the industry?	5	
	— piracy		2
	— antipathy of Government		1
	— non-availability of quality materials		1
	— videos and T.V.		1
	— coping with advancing technology		1

Note: Question (Q) followed by responses (R), the no. of respondents to that question (N) and frequency giving that response (F).

TABLE 18: Responses of the Artists to the 20 Scaled Items of Questionnaire 3 (N – 11)

		SA	A	U	D	SD		
1.	The importance of phonogram as a medium of cultural communication is very well recognised by the industry as well as the public.	6	2	2	1	-	8	1
2.	The primary intention of the recording companies as far as I know is the promotion of artists and styles of music.	-	2	2	4	3	2	7
3.	Recording companies should make maximum use of the talents of the popular and established artists rather than going for new and younger artists.	-	2	-	6	3	2	9
4.	Promoting younger and new artists involves great financial risk and hence should be done discreetly.	1	4	1	4	1	5	5
5.	The system of exclusive contract with a particular company for a definite period of time should be discontinued.	1	5	5	-	-	6	-
6.	Artists should be free to sing for any company they like.	4	7	-	-	-	11	-
7.	Artists can be paid royalty on every record/cassette sold even without entering into exclusive contract with the company.	1	5	3	1	1	6	2
8.	The recording companies keep very good relationship with their artistes.	2	3	4	-	2	5	2
9.	Recording companies take special take special care of those artists who are under exclusive contract with their companies.	-	4	2	4	1	4	5
10.	Recording companies are concerned about the personal well-being of the artists.	1	2	1	4	3	3	7
11.	Remuneration given by the recording companies is reasonable.	-	3	5	1	2	3	3
12.	The company officials are faithful in matters of payment of royalty.	-	2	3	5	6	2	6
13.	Royalty rates should be the same for all artists irrespective of their popularity and prestige.	1	3	2	3	2	4	5
14.	There should be uniform royalty rates for all companies.	2	4	1	4	-	6	4
15.	Flat payment for each programme at the time of recording is better than royalty payments.	3	4	3	1	-	7	1

16. Recording artists must have an association of their own.

    7 3 - 1 -
    10 1

17. The recent "Cassette Boom" has adversely affected the number of live programmes and the number of participants for these programmes.

    1 1 2 5 2
    2 7

18. There should be less number of recording companies doing more organised business than more companies doing less organised business.

    1 4 1 4 1
    5 5

19. There is a mushroom growth of recording organisation in the country because the organised companies have failed to meet the requirements of the consumers.

    2 4 1 4 -
    6 4

20. The artists share equal responsibility with the industry in fighting against piracy and other unauthorised reproduction of recorded programmes.

    7 3 - - 1
    10 1

Explanation: The lower figures under main frequencies of SA, A, U, D, SD are the frequencies when the two points of Agreement or Disagreement are combined to convert the 5-point scale into a 3-point scale. This is done to indicate the trend of responses more clearly, as often the finer discrimination needed for a 5-point marking may not be possible and two points may overlap.

BIBLIOGRAPHY

Barnouw, Erik and S. Krishnaswamy, (1980), *Indian cinema* 2nd edition, Oxford University Press, New Delhi.

Basu, Debashis, (1985), His Master's feeble voice, *Update* 3 (12) 14 June.

Beaud, Paul (1977), Methodologische Probleme, In Blaukopf, Kurt, *Massenmedium Schallplatte*, Breitkopf & Hartel, Wiesbaden.

———, (1982), Statistics and methodology, In Blaukopf, Kurt, *The Phonogram in cultural communication*, Springer-Verlag, Wien and New York.

Blaukopf, Kurt, (1977), *Massenmedium Schallplatte*, Breitkopf & Härtel, Wiesbaden.

———, (1982), *The phonogram in cultural communication*, Springer-Verlag, Wien and New York.

———, (1985), Strategies of music industries and radio organisations, *Final report* of the Project No. 11, Promotion of Creativity taking into account the development of the Culture Industries, Council for Cultural Relations, Strasbourg.

Comper, Denis, (1977), A century of sound recording, *Journal of the National Centre for the Performing Arts*, VI(3), from *Unesco Features*.

Danielou, Alain, (1952), *Catalogue of Indian music*, referred in Jaap Kunst, *Ethnomusicology*, Unesco, Paris.

Expanding repertoire, In *Sounds of music - 71* feature of *Screen*, 8 March, 1985.

Eye Spy, (1985), Multi-nationals again, *Trade Guide*, 27 July.

Ghosh, Saroj, (1985) as quoted in a news item, India: a festival of Science, reported in *Times of India*, Delhi, 6 November.

Gronow, Pekka, (1981), The record industry comes to the orient, *Ethnomusicology*, 25 (2), May.

IFPI (1983), Extent of piracy of sound recordings worldwide in 1982, (Brochure), IFPI Secretariat, London.

Joshi, G.M. (1984), *Down Melody Lane*, Orient Longman, Hyderabad.

Joshi G.N. (1977), The phonograph in India, *Journal of the National Centre for the Performing Arts*, VI (3), September.

Kuckreja, Shekhar, (1984), *The problems of the music industry in India and the remedial measures required to rejuvenate it*, Project report, DMM.

Kumar, Hemanta (1985), No takers for slow music: an interview by Kaberi Basu, *Hindustan Times*, Sunday Magazine, 11 August.

Kunst, Jaap, (1959), *Ethnomusicology*, 3rd edition, Martinus Nijhoff, The Hague.

Malm, Krister, (1984), Phonograms and Cultural policy in Sweden, *The Phonogram in Cultural Communication*, in Blaukopf, Kurt, (ed), Springer - Verlag, Wien and New York.

News (1985), Suit against Gramophone Co., *Film Information*, 24 August.

Ojha J.M. (1984), *Culture, Cultural Behaviour and Tourism*: Presidential address to the Section of Psychology and Educational Sciences of the Indian Science Congress. 71st session at Ranchi.

—— (1985), *Media as an important determinant of the cultural ecology of the Indian people*: paper presented at the Seminar, 'Media, Culture, Life Styles', at Mediacult, Vienna, (April).

Raghavan V. (1953), *The present state of music education in the Asiatic continent*: an exposé presented during the 3rd plenary session of the International Conference on Musical Education, at Brussels, (2 July).

Raghavan V. (1984), Electronics Information and Planning. *Report of the Study Team on Consumer electronics industry*, 11 (12) September.

Raghavan V. (1985), Tribute to Indira, in *'Sounds of Music - 71'* feature of *Screen*, (8 March).

Unesco, (1984), *Copyright Bulletin*, Special issue, xviii (2).

Wallis, Roger and Krister Malm (1984), *Big Sounds from Small Peoples*, Constable, London.

INDEX

CICIL LIST

CONCEPTS IN COMMUNICATION, INFORMATICS & LIBRARIANSHIP (CICIL)

General Editor: S.P. AGRAWAL

CICIL-1 Development of Library Services in India: Social Science Information
S.P. Agrawal Rs. 150

CICIL-2 Development of Documentation in India: Social Science Information
S.P. Agrawal Rs. 250

CICIL-3 UNESCO and Social Sciences: Retrospect and Prospect
S.P. Agrawal and **J.C. Aggarwal** Rs. 250

CICIL-4 INDIANA : A Bibliography of Bibliographical Sources
M.K. Jain Rs. 200

CICIL-5 Dimensions of Library and Information Science: Kaula Festschrift
V. Venkatappaiah (Eds.) Rs. 600

CICIL-6 Book Numbers: Some Indian Methods
M.P. Satija and **S.P. Agrawal** Rs. 100

CICIL-7 National Policy for University Libraries in India: Problems and Perspectives
N.B. Inamdar and **L.S. Ramaiah** (Ed.) Rs. 250

CICIL-8 Media Utilisation for the Development of Women and Children
B.S. Thakur and **Binod C. Agrawal** Rs. 150

CICIL-9 Terrorism: An Annotated Bibliography
Susheela Bhan (Ed.) Rs. 275

CICIL-10 Transnational Library Relations: The Indo-American Experience
M.B. Konnur Rs. 175

CICIL-11 Geography of Marketing and Commercial Activities in India (Documentation on Research Information)
R.S. Dixit Rs. 130

CICIL-12 Information India 1988: Global View
S.P. Agrawal and **J.C. Aggarwal** Rs. 200

CICIL-13 Women's Education in India: Historical Review, Present Status and Perspective Plan
S.P. Agrawal and **J.C. Aggarwal** Rs. 360

CICIL-14 Cultural Communication in India: Role and Impact of Phonograms
J.M. Ojha (in press)

CICIL-15 Second Historical Survey of Educational Development in India: Select Documents 1985-1989
S.P. Agrawal and **J.C. Aggarwal** Rs. 490

CICIL-16 Documentation Encyclopaedia of UNESCO and Education
J.C. Aggarwal and **S.P. Agrawal** Rs. 800 (set of 2 parts)

CICIL-17 Attitude Towards Information: A Study of Post-Graduate Teachers and Researchers in Social Sciences
N.G. Satish (in press)

CICIL-18 Librarianship and Bureaucratic Organisation: A Study in the Sociology of Library Profession in India
P.K. Jayaswal Rs. 175

CICIL-19 Literature Search
K.A. Isaac Rs. 150

CICIL-20 Child Education in India: Index to Scholarly Writings in Indian Educational Journals and Newspapers since independence
S.P. Agrawal and **Naresh Kanta** Rs. 100

CICIL-21 Lok Sabha and Vidhan Sabha Elections in India 1989 & 1990: Process and Results with Comparative Study of Manifestos
S.P. Agrawal and **J.C. Aggarwal** Rs. 250

CICIL-22 Islamic Studies in India: A Survey of Human, Institutional and Documentary Sources
Mohamed Taher Rs. 180

CICIL-23 Panchayati Raj: An Annotated Bibliography
N.B. Inamdar, N.G. Satish and **Anil Takalkar** 290

CICIL-24 Information India 1989-90: Global View
S.P. Agrawal and **J.C. Aggarwal** Rs. 500

CICIL-25 First Handbook of Psychological and Social Instruments
Udai Pareek and **T. Venkateswara Rao** (in press)

CICIL-26 Educational and Social Uplift of Backward Classes: At What Cost and How? Mandal Commission and After
S.P. Agrawal and **J.C. Aggarwal** Rs. 275

CICIL-27 Mass Media and New Horizons: Impact of TV & Video an Urban Milieu
H.R. Trivedi Rs. 180

CICIL-28 Indian Writings on Education : An Indicator to Indian Educational Journals Grouped by Subject Deseriptors 1979 to 1986 (in two parts)
S.P. Agarwal Rs. 900 (per set)

CICIL-29 Nation in Crisis
S.P. Agrawal and **J.C. Aggarwal** Rs. 200

CICIL-30 Information India 1990-91: Global View
S.P. Agrawal and **J.C. Aggarwal** Rs. 500

CICIL-31 Development of University Libraries in India After Independence
O.P. Gupta Rs. 270

CICIL-32 Handbook on Child : With Historical Background
Pramila Pandit Barooah Rs. 320

CICIL-33 Weaker Section in Indian Society : Undiscovered Past, Uncertain Present and Unpredictable Future Index to Writings in Indian Scholarly Journals and 10 National Newspapers Classified under 1500 Descriptors 1886-1990
S.P. Agrawal and **Rajeev Kumar Sharma** Rs. 600

CICIL-34 Communication Informatics and Librarianship in India : An Introductory Guide to Publications Based on a Survey of Libraries in Capital of City India
S.P. Agrawal and **Pushpa Rani Sharma** Rs. 720

CICIL-35 Problems of Collection Development in Special Libraries
M.S. Sridhar Rs. 225

CICIL-36 National Information Resources for Social Sciences in India : Mobilisation, Dispersal and International Enhancement
S.P. Agrawal Rs. 225